D1572395

Praise for *Finding God in Suffering*

"I wish I didn't need this book, but I do. We all do, because so much of life is occupied with suffering— grief, disappointment, physical pain, shame. Jesus Christ showed us the way through every ordeal, empowering us not only to endure, but to triumph. In these pages, Father Mahar shows us that way, helping us to understand it as he provides clear, practical spiritual guidance."

— Mike Aquilina, executive vice-president,
St. Paul Center for Biblical Theology;
author, *The Fathers of the Church*; EWTN host

"Suffering is often opposed to human happiness, and its incidence often robs life of its meaning. In *Finding God in Suffering*, Father Mahar evangelizes the human experience of suffering, illustrating how it can serve God's purpose and is, therefore, not a sign of the absence of God."

— Cardinal Peter Turkson, Chancellor,
Pontifical Academies for Sciences and Social Sciences

"Despite the 'broken families, broken promises, and broken lives' all around us, [Father Christopher Mahar] effectively illustrates the astonishing Good News of our faith—that the 'Gospel of Suffering' allows every trial to be a rich encounter with Christ and an opportunity to embrace a creative vocation radiating hope."

— Genevieve Kineke, author and speaker
on authentic Catholic femininity

"Finding an answer to the question of suffering is one of the most crucial discoveries in life. Father Mahar masterfully and gracefully guides us into this difficult subject, helps us to find God in suffering, and in him discover its meaning and value. This work is an answer to the prayers and cries of so many presently in dark valleys, and it is a source of light and hope to all those who compassionately strive to love and care for them."

— Father Roger Landry, Catholic Chaplain,
Columbia University.

"The shadow of the Cross falls upon each of us in different ways and can plunge us into disorientating darkness, distress, and even despair. *Where is God?* we ask.

"Yet, for the Christian, the Cross is a sign of hope: its deepest shadows are cast by the light of Easter morning. The victory of Our Lord Jesus Christ over sin and death transforms our suffering and gives it redemptive value. In our suffering and through it we can participate in that victory; we can encounter God with an intimacy and purity of heart perhaps hitherto unknown.

"Pope Benedict XVI taught, 'Suffering accepted for love of Christ, for love of God and of others is a redeeming force, a force of love.' May Father Christopher Mahar's profound book help us to retrieve this power, this force of love, which is so often absent in the suffering of men and women today. May it inspire each of us always to persevere in the supernatural hope that suffering borne for the love of God betokens, for, as Our Lord taught, 'He who perseveres to the end shall be saved' (Mt 24:13)."

— Robert Cardinal Sarah, Prefect Emeritus
of the Congregation for Divine Worship
and Discipline of the Sacraments.

FINDING GOD
IN SUFFERING

FINDING GOD IN SUFFERING

By Father Christopher M. Mahar

auline
BOOKS & MEDIA
Boston

Library of Congress Control Number: 2023934139

ISBN 10: 0-8198-2756-8
ISBN 13: 978-0-8198-2756-2

Every effort has been made to trace copyright holders and to obtain their permission for the use of copyright material. The publisher apologizes for any errors or omissions in the above list and would be grateful if notified of any corrections that should be incorporated in future reprints or editions of this book.

Cover design by Ryan McQuade
Cover art and frontispiece: *The Crowning with Thorns*, Caravaggio (Kunsthistorisches Museum, Vienna, wikicommons).

Excerpts of the *Catechism of the Catholic Church* are taken from the English translation for use in the United States of America copyright © 1994, United States Conference of Catholic Bishops—Libreria Editrice Vaticana. English translation of the *Catechism of the Catholic Church: Modifications from the Editio Typica*, copyright © 1997, United States Conference of Catholic Bishops—Libreria Editrice Vaticana.

Published by Pauline Books & Media, 50 Saint Paul's Avenue, Boston, MA 02130-3491

Printed in the U.S.A.

www.pauline.org

Pauline Books & Media is the publishing house of the Daughters of St. Paul, an international congregation of women religious serving the Church with the communications media.

1 2 3 4 5 6 7 8 9   28 27 26 25 24 23

To my parents, Earl and Mary,
and my siblings, Melissa and Matthew.

Contents

Part I

When We Suffer

Part II

How We Suffer

Appendices

Salvific Suffering

A Redeeming Force

It was the Great Jubilee Year 2000 and I was a seminarian standing in St. Peter's Square. Saint John Paul II was celebrating Mass as I shuffled uncomfortably and tried to understand the homily. The Pope's words were labored and, at certain points, incoherent. The Parkinson's disease that he had endured for so long had taken its toll, but it did not hinder him from addressing the crowd of pilgrims that day. He was speaking about suffering and discipleship, subjects that interested me a great deal. In many ways it was the experience of the cross that had led me to a deeper understanding of God in my life. Through the conflicts I faced in my daily life, I had come to discover that Christ, who willingly took up his cross, desires to draw near to us when we endure difficulties and challenges. Listening now to the Pope addressing suffering, I found that his words rang with a magnetic authenticity.

The Mass continued, and at one point my attention was drawn to the jumbotron as the camera closed in on him. He was holding his crosier, the large staff that symbolized his governance and shepherding care of God's flock. At the top of the crosier was the crucifix graphically depicting the wounded and suffering Christ. Undoubtedly his own life had come to resemble the Lord's cross more and more through the accumulation of sufferings he had experienced. As the image remained on the screen for some time, I was flushed with emotion and thought, *"This is the homily he was preaching moments ago."* The messenger was himself the message.

In that same place, on a warm and sunny day in May of 1981, Pope Saint John Paul II had survived an attempt on his life that left the world in shock. The following Sunday, from his room in the Policlinico Gemelli hospital, he sent a brief, pre-recorded message to be played for vigilant pilgrims in St. Peter's: "I pray for that brother of ours who shot me, and whom I have sincerely pardoned. United with Christ, priest and victim, I offer my sufferings for the Church and for the world."[1] To hear the voice of the fallen Pope speaking anew to his flock was itself a triumph, but those words carried a profound and even daunting message that still awaited further expression and a deeper explanation.

Nearly three years later, on the Memorial of Our Lady of Lourdes, patroness of the sick, the Holy Father gave the Church and the world the Apostolic Letter *Salvifici Doloris*, "On the Christian Meaning of Human Suffering." One man's personal struggle with evil and the cross would become a gift

---

1. *L'Osservatore Romano*, English weekly edition, no. 20 (Vatican), May 18, 1981.

for those immersed in what he described as the "world of suffering."[2]

The cross, in one form or another, enters into every human life. For some, it may seem overwhelming, a weight almost too heavy to bear. For other people, perhaps there are several, lesser burdens, but ones that last for long periods of time. Big or small, many or few, we all bear them. What Saint John Paul II teaches the Church and the world is that we are not alone in our struggle. There are answers from God, even in the midst of suffering. He who began his pontificate with an encyclical letter on Christ the Redeemer directs our gaze to the Lord of all, who has the power to transform even sorrow and pain into hope and new life.

In the sufferings that Saint John Paul II bore throughout his life, which were pronounced and widely visible at his life's end, he taught us that there is meaning in suffering and that God draws near to those who struggle beneath the burden of the cross. Pope Benedict XVI, describing the ailing Saint John Paul II, explained how "he showed us that suffering accepted for love of Christ, for love of God and of others is a redeeming force, a force of love and no less powerful than the great deeds he accomplished in the first part of his Pontificate."[3]

This book is inspired by both the messenger, Saint John Paul II, and the message of redemptive suffering that he

---

2. Saint John Paul II, *Salvifici Doloris: On the Christian Meaning of Human Suffering* (Boston: Pauline Books and Media, 1984), no. 8.

3. Pope Benedict XVI, "Meeting of the Holy Father Benedict XVI with the Clergy of the Diocese of Bolzano-Bressanone," The Holy See, August 6, 2008, http://w2.vatican.va/content/benedict-xvi/en/speeches/2008/august/documents/hf_ben-xvi_spe_20080806_clero-bressanone.html

teaches us in *Salvifici Doloris*. In many ways the chapters of this book follow the questions, challenges, and themes of that apostolic letter. Each chapter, therefore, builds upon the material that comes before it and helps to form a composite of the complex and compelling reality of human suffering.

While we all struggle to find an answer to the question of suffering in our own lives, the solution is not so simple. The *Catechism of the Catholic Church* explains that "only the Christian faith as a whole constitutes the answer to this question."[4] Our faith celebrates the amazing story of the God who created us in love and sent Christ into the world to find us when we became lost; in the most dramatic of ways Christ underwent the passion to redeem us and founded the Church to embrace the world with his message of salvation. This integral drama alone has the capacity to address the difficult and often overwhelming question of suffering. The chapters of this book attempt to unfold that drama and allow the reader to understand that God will stop at nothing to communicate his redemptive and healing love to those who suffer.

Finding God in Suffering is written with the individual person in mind and can serve as a personal guide through what may seem at times to be a labyrinth of suffering. It might also be helpful to read this book in groups, leaning on the assistance of others who can share our burden of suffering and help us to find the strength to move forward in faith.

---

4. *Catechism of the Catholic Church*, 2nd ed. (Washington, DC: United States Catholic Conference, Inc.—Libreria Editrice Vaticana, 1997), no. 309.

In the chapters that follow, there are many different stories of suffering and of healing. Some are compelling anecdotes or tales from the lives of the saints; others are taken from literature. All of the stories are intended to help the reader enter more deeply into the greatest story ever told: the drama of the eternal Son of God who loved us and offered his life for us on Calvary.

What the teachings of our faith propose, and what the witness and writings of Saint John Paul II articulate, is not merely that there is a meaning in human suffering. More than that, they communicate the profound and mysterious truth that, even in suffering, we can find love. They present nothing less than this astounding paradox: in the cross of Jesus Christ, love has found us.

Part I

When We Suffer

Chapter i

The Encounter with Suffering

Diagnosing the Disease

Kristin sits uncomfortably on the cold paper sheet that covers the cushioned examination table in her doctor's office. The preliminary evaluation is over. She waits for the physician with mixed emotions: fear, impatience, resignation. In the last few weeks she has experienced several surprising episodes: tightness in her throat, shortness of breath, and the terrible feeling that she was going to be sick. It happened twice in the supermarket, and then again during a meeting at work. Something was wrong. Was it the onset of some terrible and debilitating illness?

She has explained it all to her doctor, who listened with careful attention and asked many questions. Some of them were about her health, while others seemed more personal.

Oddly, she felt relieved responding to inquiries about her increased responsibilities at work and challenges at home that were weighing heavily upon her.

Finally, her physician returns and takes a seat beside the examination table. Kristin is fighting back tears, convinced that this will be very bad news. "Everything looks great so far," the doctor says. "There are no major concerns." Kristin sighs, expressing both relief and confusion. The doctor goes on to explain that Kristin may be suffering from increased anxiety and something called agoraphobia. She smiles and hands Kristin a small booklet with that strange name on the cover. "Let's start with this," she says. "We'll call it homework for your health. It's a different kind of medicine, but it has proven very helpful for the very thing you are struggling with. Look it over, and we can check back in a few weeks." Kristin takes the booklet home and reads it, feeling consoled by the descriptions detailing her own personal experience. She is still facing a difficult climb. It is not the last time she will struggle with anxiety, but now that she knows more about what she is up against, her response from this point forward will be different, better.

Reading a book on suffering will not remove our difficulties and crosses any more than a booklet on agoraphobia will take away anxiety. But knowing more about suffering, and reflecting on the insights of the saints and the teachings of our faith, can help us to see what we are up against. More than that, we come to discover that we are not alone.

The experience of suffering is universal, indiscriminate, and often devastatingly cruel. Suffering can occur instantaneously or accumulate over time. It can manifest itself in a single moment or last for several years. Suffering can quickly lead to a sense of isolation as it generates conflict within our physical and spiritual lives, with those around us, and even with our understanding of the meaning of life. Thus, the world of human suffering, says Saint John Paul II, is a highly personal one in which "suffering seems almost inexpressible and not transferable."[5] One of the first non-starters counselors are taught to avoid is the platitude, "I know how you feel." You don't.

Within the experience of isolation and disorientation, "there inevitably arises *the question: Why?*"[6] We often ask questions such as: Why is God allowing this to happen? Why is this taking place at this time in my life? Why am I suffering in this way?

Suffering may even challenge our belief in a good and loving God. In the opening part of the *Summa Theologica*, Saint Thomas Aquinas frames the argument with blunt precision: "The word 'God' means that He is infinite goodness. If, therefore, God existed, there would be no evil discoverable; but there is evil in the world. Therefore God does not exist."[7] At the surface, the argument seems somewhat simplistic. Aquinas himself will go on to refute it handily, offering several of his famous "proofs" for the existence of God. On a personal level, however, the case against God's

---

5. Saint John Paul II, *Salvifici Doloris*, no. 5.

6. Saint John Paul II, *Salvifici Doloris*, no. 9.

7. Saint Thomas Aquinas, *Summa Theologica*, trans. Fathers of the English Dominican Province (New York: Benzinger Brothers, 1948), 1, Q. 2, A. 3.

existence in the face of human suffering often gains surprising strength. Philosophical propositions do not always motivate us. Pain does.

When we try to make sense of suffering, we are not seeking scientific data nor analyzing the physical symptoms of some puzzling illness. What we are seeking is something much more innate and proper to humanity itself. In *Salvifici Doloris*, Saint John Paul II says that a more complete picture emerges when we are able to perceive the distinction between physical suffering and moral suffering.[8] Physical suffering can accompany any of a number of illnesses and ailments, from chronic back pain to cancer. Another form of suffering related to the body is psychological suffering, which encompasses the entire spectrum of mental illness, from clinical depression to crippling neuroses.

Moral suffering, however, is different. Saint John Paul II describes moral suffering as "pain of the soul."[9] There is no prescription to alleviate that affliction; no therapy or surgery will correct or mitigate it. Moral suffering is pain of a spiritual nature. Witnessing a grave error in judgment or ethics in a leader or a revered family member could result in a moral injury; we may feel a sense of betrayal when we become the victim of another person's transgressions. Likewise, we often suffer spiritual consequences for the sins that we freely commit. Moral suffering, in other words, produces a wound that is felt deep within the soul.

Recognizing the difference between physical suffering and moral suffering is important, because we are created by

---

8. Saint John Paul II, *Salvifici Doloris*, no. 5.

9. Saint John Paul II, *Salvifici Doloris*, no. 5.

God as human persons, body and soul. God can and does speak to us through the sufferings that we experience and helps us to become aware of our need not for just a medical remedy but for the Divine Physician, Jesus Christ.

When suffering enters into our lives, it is perceived as an offense. This is personal. We rise up and protest because it is something keenly felt, and on a much deeper level than the merely physical. What we encounter when we come face to face with suffering is an experience of negativity. In a word, "Man suffers whenever he experiences any kind of evil."[10]

1. Where has suffering entered into my life? How has it touched my family or community?

2. Have I honestly confronted God with the question of "Why?" What kinds of fears can hold me back?

3. Where have I gone to seek a "remedy" for the wounds I have received in the past? Where do I desire to go in the future?

O GOD, YOU CREATED us in love and made us for yourself. Our bodies and souls are a gift from you and you direct our lives so that we may share in your love and your life. In those places where we feel the wounds of the brokenness of this world, give us your strength and the healing that we long for. Help us to recognize you in the midst of our pain, and to know that you are near. We ask this in the name of Jesus Christ, our Lord. Amen.

---

10. Saint John Paul II, *Salvifici Doloris*, no. 7.

CHAPTER 2

The Problem of Evil

Distortion of the Good

They call it "ground zero." It is the precise place where a nuclear explosion impacts the surface of the earth. On August 6, 1945, three days after the bombing of Hiroshima, an atomic bomb was dropped on Nagasaki, Japan. The blast killed an estimated sixty thousand people, adding to the forty million civilian casualties already experienced in World War II. One of the youngest survivors of the Nagasaki bombing was Joseph Mitsuaki Takami, whose mother was pregnant with him at the time. Joseph was born seven months later and went on to pursue seminary studies as he discerned the call of God. He was ordained a Catholic priest in 1972. Saint John Paul II appointed him Archbishop of Nagasaki in 2003. He is an outspoken opponent of nuclear armament, having lived in the shadow of "ground zero" and witnessed its disastrous effects.

Another unlikely "survivor" of the Nagasaki blast is a statue of Saint Agnes from the Cathedral of the Immaculate Conception. Covered in the debris from that leveled church, which had stood half a kilometer from Nagasaki's "ground zero," that statue was driven deep enough below the surface during the initial blast that it was shielded from the intense heat and radiation emanating from the explosion. Today it stands in the United Nations Headquarters in New York City, a reminder not only of the futility and destructiveness of war, but of the faith and hope that endure through the fires of adversity.

The term "ground zero," sadly, is not restricted to the nuclear destruction of Hiroshima and Nagasaki. It has been used to describe natural disasters like the 2004 tsunami in Indonesia, as well as the terrorist attacks at New York City on September 11, 2001. "Ground zero" is the point of impact, the place where tragedy has struck. It can be as devastating for an individual as for a nation. "Ground zero" is a phone call in the middle of the night. It is an unexpected medical diagnosis. It could be a failed marriage, a broken relationship, or the loss of a job. Suddenly things in our lives have changed and we are left wondering what went wrong.

Saint John Paul II insists that suffering is always caused by an experience of evil, which he defines as "a certain lack, limitation or distortion of the good."[11] Here he expresses clearly the traditional Catholic theology of evil as something always in relation to a good. We suffer when we do not have

---

11. Saint John Paul II, *Salvifici Doloris*, no. 7.

something we ought to have, when there is a lack of some legitimate good that has somehow been denied us. Peace and stability break down, resulting in war and destruction. A body that once exuded health and vigor is painfully compromised and now becomes the source of personal conflict. Maybe promises were made, vows exchanged, and instead of a shared happiness there is isolation and loneliness. When God created humanity, he declared that it was "very good" (Genesis 1:31). He created us *for* the good. When that intention is not realized, we suffer. God's plan and the desire of the human heart are frustrated by evil.

The limitation and distortion of the good threatens much more than our personal happiness, though. While technology and science can often provide a more humane and sustainable existence, humanity has not always continued to advance on an ethical level. Saint John Paul II, who witnessed the destruction of his homeland in World War II and lived through its aftermath, speaks of "*an incomparable accumulation of sufferings*, even to the possible self-destruction of humanity."[12] He was referring specifically to the threat of nuclear war, but we can also think about the painful reality of what Pope Francis has referred to as the "Third World War fought in pieces."[13] There are so many places in the world today where peace is a far cry from the human experience and destruction has wreaked havoc on homeland and family life.

---

12. Saint John Paul II, *Salvifici Doloris*, no. 8.

13. "Celebration Presided over by Pope Francis at the Military Memorial of Redipuglia on the Occasion of the 100th Anniversary of the Outbreak of the First World War," September 13, 2014, https://www.vatican.va/content/francesco/en/homilies/2014/documents/papa-francesco_20140913_omelia-sacrario-militare-redipuglia.html.

Whether we experience evil personally or perceive its threatening presence on a global scale, there can be no doubt that it leaves us vulnerable. Evil exposes the underbelly of humanity, and it is often accompanied by a disarming sense of our utter dependence. When we suffer and experience evil, we recognize all too well our shortcomings, our frailty, and our need for help. It is then, perhaps, that we are more open to assistance and help from God and those around us. We are finite, and nothing wakes us up to this reality more than suffering. C. S. Lewis describes the surprising, even positive implications of our vulnerability in terms of Christian faith. He notes how a recognition of our limitations, and even the painful reality of suffering, can become an opening for something else:

> If the first and lowest operation of pain shatters the illusion that all is well, the second shatters the illusion that what we have, whether good or bad in itself, is our own and enough for us. Everyone has noticed how hard it is to turn our thoughts to God when everything is going well with us. We "have all we want" is a terrible saying when "all" does not include God. [14]

Lewis is not naïve or callous in suggesting that God uses pain to speak to us. He acknowledges that pain, what he calls "God's megaphone,"[15] could also lead to bitterness and a rejection of God. What is important here is that pain can, and often does, draw our attention to a wider and more complex reality outside of ourselves. It would be incorrect to assume

---

14. C. S. Lewis, *The Problem of Pain* (New York: Macmillan, 1962), 95–96.

15. Lewis, *The Problem of Pain*, 93.

that God allows suffering just to get our attention, but pain does have the capacity to set us on a path outward.

Saint Augustine reminds us that our hearts are restless until they rest in God. It is the restless heart in the throes of suffering that seeks, and perhaps even demands, to discover the reasons behind the conflicts of everyday life. Time and again, we are driven by the sense that there must be more to suffering than we have yet been able to grasp. It is not enough for us to recognize that we are experiencing some lack or limitation of a good we ought to have. Instead, we want to know why. What we are searching for, ultimately, is meaning.

1. Have I experienced a "ground zero" moment in my life? Have such moments in the world around me affected my life and relationships?

2. Where do I see a lack or distortion of the good in the world around me? What is my initial reaction to this evil? What is the response I want to have?

3. What are some ways I can invite God into the midst of the emptiness and pain in my life?

O GOD, ALMIGHTY FATHER, our lives are often fragile and vulnerable to the tragic moments of evil and sorrow that can happen in our world. It can be so difficult to find you in the darkness when everything seems to be moving in the wrong direction. Help us to recognize that you are present in our lives and calling out to us in our loneliness and pain. You are the light shining in our darkness. May we always place our faith, hope, and love in you. We ask this in the name of Jesus Christ, our Lord. Amen.

CHAPTER 3

Transcendence and Hope

The Search for Meaning

The prisoners were led out of the camp on a forced march. It was pitch black, several hours before the breaking of dawn. Whenever the cold, biting wind subsided, they could hear the shouting of the guards. Like cattle they were driven along the frozen gravel path leading to the work site. They held on to each other desperately for support, stumbling forward in the darkness. Suddenly Viktor Frankl heard the muffled voice of the prisoner next to him. Speaking furtively into his upturned collar, he said, "If our wives could see us now!"[16] Our wives . . .

Frankl had married Tilly in the winter of 1941. Within a year, they had been deported to a concentration camp in

---

16. Viktor E. Frankl, *Man's Search for Meaning* (Boston: Beacon Press, 1985), 56.

German-occupied Czechoslovakia. Two years after that they were moved to Auschwitz, and it was there that they were separated. He had not seen her since. Where was she now? The thought of her kept crashing in as he pressed on in the cold beneath the stars.

Gradually the black sky above them gave way to a soft pink, and then spread out into a warm orange glow. If our wives could see us now . . . Frankl had not been expecting to see beauty when the day began. Now he was surrounded by its radiance. The image of Tilly came clearly into his mind, as vivid as if she had been standing before him. He could almost hear her voice, could see the lines move across her face as she smiled. Years later, after the camp was liberated, Frankl would reflect on that remarkable morning:

> A thought transfixed me: for the first time in my life I saw the truth as it is set into song by so many poets, proclaimed as the final wisdom by so many thinkers. The truth—that love is the ultimate and the highest goal to which man can aspire. Then I grasped the meaning of the greatest secret that human poetry and human thought and belief have to impart: The salvation of man is through love and in love. I understand how a man who has nothing left in this world may still know bliss, be it only for a brief moment, in the contemplation of his beloved.[17]

✠ ✠ ✠

In the spring of 1945, Viktor Frankl returned to his native Austria and began to lecture widely on the search for meaning,

---

17. Frankl, *Man's Search for Meaning*, 57.

what he explained as a primary motivation for life. His personal account of the war and the insights he discovered amid unspeakable horror were recorded in his landmark bestseller, *Man's Search for Meaning*. If there is any meaning at all to the question of suffering, Frankl discovered, then it must come from outside of the one who suffers. No less than a sunrise or a vivid memory of the beloved, suffering can orient the soul outward. There is an earnest determination within the human spirit that stubbornly seeks to understand the reasons and purpose behind the misfortunes of life. Dehumanizing and debilitating as human suffering may be, it is also something that belongs to our transcendence.

When we suffer we look for a way out, some chance of escape or release from the confines of the reality that has come upon us. Hope is the virtue that spurs us to seek that freedom from outside of ourselves. It is one of the three theological virtues, along with faith and love, that places us directly in relationship with the living God.

Saint John of the Cross teaches that the virtue of hope, as much as it relates to our desire to see things work out well in the future, is actually rooted in the past. He says that hope is located in the memory. When we *remember* the fidelity of God in so many of the difficult experiences of the past, we can have hope that this same God will be with us in the present moment and will guide us on into the future.

There is a compelling story of hope found in the Old Testament in the First Book of Samuel. Israel is in great affliction at the hands of the Philistines. To add insult to injury, a great warrior named Goliath has come out against the army of Israel to taunt them. He challenges them to send one man to meet him on the battlefield and settle the matter for good. An unassuming shepherd boy named David accepts the challenge. Saul, Israel's king, is impressed by the courage of this young man but is doubtful that David can win in the fight against Goliath. David responds by saying that he has served his father for many years as a shepherd, and that sometimes lions and bears would attack the flock. In those times the Lord had always helped David to defend the innocent lambs, and he insists that the same God will not fail him now. "The LORD who delivered me from the paw of the lion and the paw of the bear," he says to King Saul, "will deliver me from the hand of this Philistine" (1 Samuel 17:37).

Many times when we suffer, we may feel that we are up against Goliath and that we are outmatched and helpless to change our lot. Hope teaches us a different lesson. We need only to search our memory to draw strength from the fact that God is faithful and will never forsake us. God is the same "yesterday and today and for ever" (Hebrews 13:8). Even in times of darkness and distress, when it is difficult to connect with the fruitfulness of the past—or even if our past is full of memories of intense suffering—we can be buoyed by the fidelity of God in stories such as David's, or in the lives of those around us. God's merciful love is constantly at work in our loved ones, in the lives of believers everywhere, and in the lives of the saints. We need not look too far to discover the light of hope that has the power to dispel the darkness.

The hope we find in God's transcendence, however, will not take away all our problems. Suffering, in fact, remains a mystery even when we can recognize that God is present. The Catholic philosopher Gabriel Marcel offers a famous distinction between a problem and a mystery. A problem, he explains, is something which we can confront, lay siege to, and reduce to our own terms. We can solve a problem. Mystery is different. Mystery, he says, "is something in which I myself am involved" and therefore "by definition, transcends every conceivable technique."[18] The mystery of suffering defies every human attempt to solve it or figure it out. God, however, teaches us that mystery opens the heart to the transcendent, and he reminds us that we are never alone when we suffer. God himself is a mystery. We could never fully plumb the depths of God or fathom the sublime love that he has for us. It is precisely this love that breaks through, like a sunrise in an unexpected place, to awaken us to the truth that there is always hope.

1. Have I ever experienced a moment of transcendence in an otherwise dark period of my life? Has there been a time in my suffering when God's presence broke through?

2. How might God be inviting me to grow in the virtue of hope? How can I live out the virtue of hope in a practical way in my life at this time?

3. How has God been faithful to me in the past? Can I recall any particular moments when his hand guided me and helped me to find true peace?

O GOD, ALMIGHTY FATHER, when we stumble in the darkness we often feel alone and afraid. We search for you and for some sense of comfort. Your love reminds us that long before we ever turn to you, we are already being sought after and cared for. Help us to recognize how you are present in our suffering. Give us new hope that we will never be alone because we will never be without you. We ask this in the name of Jesus Christ, our Lord. Amen.

---

18. Gabriel Marcel, *Being and Having* (London: Collins, 1965), 127.

CHAPTER 4

Castles East of Eden

Freedom's Sacred Space

Prince Caspian is the second book of C. S. Lewis' epic series, *The Chronicles of Narnia*. The Pevensie children—Peter, Susan, Edmund, and Lucy—are mystically transported from a busy train station in England to a densely wooded island in the middle of nowhere. It is not their first such experience. They had once reigned as kings and queens in the magical land of Narnia for years on end, only to return to modern-day England. Remarkably, almost no time had passed them by in England, although they had experienced decades of adventures in Narnia. Was this island now a similar adventure?

Scavenging for food, the children stumble upon an old orchard. Dozens of apple trees, shabby because uncared for, are spread out across an open field. The children are grateful that they still produce delicious fruit. Suddenly Lucy, the youngest of the four, spots a wall at the far side of the field. After closer inspection, the children realize that the wall is merely a part of what has remained of an old, ruined castle. Here is where the courtyard would have been; there, a great hall where the banquets must have taken place. Certainly, a tower had once stood on that spot where now there are only loose stones. The task of reconstructing that majestic castle comes easy to the Pevensies. After all, they themselves had lived in one just like it: Cair Paravel.

Each of the children recalls moments and events of the past, caught between melancholy and wonder as they think back on those enchanted days long ago. It is Peter, though, who begins to sense that there is something more to this place. It is not merely nostalgia for the past; something is here that they have been missing. He begins to point out aspects of the dilapidated structure that are not just similar to their castle in Narnia, but identical. Almost all at once they begin to understand. This is not some unfamiliar castle in a strange land. This is their very own Cair Paravel, or what is left of it.

✠ ✠ ✠

The Garden of Eden has been sketched by illustrators, painted by artists, and described in detail by authors in both poetry and prose. In Sacred Scripture, though, we only catch a fleeting glance. Adam and Eve enjoy that place for the span of two chapters before transgressing the commandment of God and being banished east of Eden. Replete in the books of the Bible that follow, however, are the descriptions of various foundations that were once glorious but are now destroyed.

Paradise lost is one of the threads we find woven all throughout Sacred Scripture.

The Prophet Nehemiah was a faithful Israelite living in exile when he heard of the fate of the massive wall that once surrounded Jerusalem. Its stones were reduced to rubble, its gates burned to the ground. His position as cupbearer to the Persian king gave him an opportunity to return and see the place for himself. Riding out at night, he inspected the ruined City of David in the moonlight. Deep inside him there was almost no light at all; his heart was broken.

Judas Maccabeus, in a different time, joined his brothers in battle as they defeated Israel's foes. Charged with emotion over their victory, they rode toward the Temple to sanctify it once again. When they arrived, however, "they saw the sanctuary desolate, the altar profaned, and the gates burned. In the courts they saw bushes sprung up as in a thicket, or as on one of the mountains. They saw also the chambers of the priests in ruins. Then they rent their clothes, and mourned with great lamentation, and sprinkled themselves with ashes" (1 Maccabees 4:38–39).

The external signs that we live in a broken world are found on the pages of every newspaper and featured daily on the evening news. G. K. Chesterton contended that simple observation of the world could demonstrate the reality of original sin. We experience its effects in our own relationships and often come to terms with the consequences of that reality as we struggle through the complexities of life. In the dramatic telling of the sin of our first parents, Adam and Eve, the Book of Genesis unveils a treasure that has too often morphed into tragedy and pain. Mysteriously but unmistakably attached to the foundations of our fallen world is the terrible abuse of human freedom.

Søren Kierkegaard, reflecting on the power of God and his ineffable goodness, insists that these very attributes are what enable human beings to possess true freedom. We too, like God, possess the power to act creatively and can willingly choose the good. God endows his creation with a sacred space of freedom. We are given liberty to choose to act along with—or, tragically, independently of—God. He intends, of course, that we choose to live creatively and responsibly, returning love for love. When we exercise our freedom in this way, we not only imitate God's creative capacity but also grow in virtue within. We become, with each new exercise of our freedom, more like the God who brought us into being in the sacred space.

When we violate that sacred space, however, and act contrary to God's commandments, we sin. Our first parents brought something into the Garden of Eden that God never intended. With that digression, they brought suffering and death into the sacred space. *Salvifici Doloris* strongly warns against the temptation to judge, with the friends of Job, that suffering has come strictly as the result of one's specific sins. Nonetheless, it also insists that "suffering cannot be divorced from the sin of the beginnings, from what Saint John calls 'the sin of the world' (John 1:29), from the sinful background of the personal actions and social processes in human history."[19]

We all have had moments when we transgressed the divine law and chose selfishness over love. The Bible offers many examples of men and women who have abused their freedom and paid the price. Adam and Eve take and eat the

---

19. Saint John Paul II, *Salvifici Doloris*, no. 15.

forbidden fruit, exchanging paradise for toil east of Eden. Their personal choice to turn away from God's plan has consequences not only for them but for all who would follow after them. David sins by taking the wife of Uriah, opening the floodgates to heartache and woe within his family and in the kingdom. The people of Israel break the covenant with God, only to languish for decades as exiles in Babylon. All of us could give similar examples—hopefully less dramatic, but perhaps just as compelling—from our own experience. Turning away from God and choosing evil can lead to great suffering, both for ourselves and those around us.

We know from experience that a failure to acknowledge the reality of sin—on a personal or social level—only increases the complex and tragic consequences so often enabled by the abuse of freedom. Archbishop Fulton Sheen often preached about sin and is known for his contention that denial of sin is a much worse spiritual fault than the sin itself. Denial of sin robs God of the ability to forgive and heal us. In the second part of his masterpiece, *Four Quartets*, T. S. Eliot addresses fallen humanity's illness and directs the reader to the only source of healing:

> Our only health is the disease
> If we obey the dying nurse
> Whose constant care is not to please
> But to remind of our, and Adam's curse,
> And that, to be restored, our sickness must grow worse.[20]

Eliot's dying nurse is the Church, instituted by Christ to announce the saving message of the Gospel. At the core of

---

20. T. S. Eliot, "East Coker," *Four Quartets*, in The Complete Poems and Plays (New York: Harcourt, Brace, 1952), 127.

that saving message is the call to repentance and the necessity
for the forgiveness that Christ died for. We begin with the
hard truth that we are sinners in need of the saving grace of
God. The sickness of sin must "grow worse" by allowing us to
see that it potentially has the power to cause death to the soul
if we are not able to access the healing power that comes to us
in Christ. Eliot continues:

> The whole earth is our hospital
> Endowed by the ruined millionaire
> Wherein, if we do well, we shall
> Die of the absolute paternal care
> That will not leave us, but prevents us everywhere.[21]

The sin of Adam, "the ruined millionaire," has left our
fallen world in a sorry state indeed. Our own sins often leave
us bankrupt and bereft. Pope Francis has often reminded the
faithful that the Church must be a field hospital, ready to bind
up the wounded and give succor to the weak and weary. "The
whole earth" is indeed our hospital, and we do well to strive
with every ounce of our energy to treat and assist those who
are vulnerable and most in need. We use our freedom to reach
out to those around us and to be the hands of God, rebuilding
the broken world that we live in. Saint Matthew's Gospel
relates the final judgment to us in precisely these terms, where
Christ identifies himself with the hungry, the thirsty, the
stranger, the naked, the sick, and those in prison and says, "As
you did it to one of the least of these my brethren, you did it
to me" (Matthew 25:40). Ultimately, the Gospel is clear that
integral health and healing are not limited to this life only.

---

21. Eliot, *Four Quartets*, 128.

The transcendent dimension is often forgotten, yet it is the final barrier to be overcome. T. S. Eliot draws us into the paradoxical reality of the Christian life, that to live one must die to self and rise with God.

It is important to note, however, that the connection between sin and suffering cannot be applied in a simple or superficial way. We see this through Sacred Scripture in a very different example of a man beset by suffering: Job. Though Job is innocent, God allows him to be tested, to be tried. He will suffer unimaginable tragedies, one after another, and for a long time, God is silent. But finally, when Job has withstood every test, God steps in to defend Job and restores all that was lost. The Book of Job holds a special place in the Old Testament anthology of suffering, for it breaks the simple mold that seeks to equate trials with transgressions. Our personal experience corroborates this. Often the innocent suffer and the meaning behind it remains hidden. Sin may provide part of the answer for why we suffer, but it cannot contain the complete meaning for the problem of suffering.

God's mysterious paternal care in our lives is never-ending, but seldom what we expect. There is hope, not for a return to the Garden of Eden, but for the rebuilding of our fallen castles and for a new heaven and a new earth where God "will wipe away every tear from their eyes, and death shall be no more" (Revelation 21:4). One thing remains clear, though, and it is that such a hope is found not in ourselves but in God. It is God who helps us to grow through suffering and to begin to make sense of the many contradictions of life. Even if we are often left with more questions than answers, we come to realize that we are not alone, because God is with us.

1. Where have I experienced the effects of sin that have brought suffering into my own life or the lives of those around me?

2. Where are some of the places that I can recognize Jesus Christ as a source of healing for myself and others?

3. How can I more fully cooperate with God in rebuilding my life and the world around me?

O GOD, ALMIGHTY FATHER, you have created us in love and given us freedom to imitate you in your goodness. Have mercy on us and help us when we misuse that freedom and turn aside from the path you have shown us. May we experience your healing touch and come to recognize the many ways you rebuild our fallen world and repair our broken lives. We ask this in the name of Jesus Christ, our Lord. Amen.

Chapter 5

Growth in Suffering

A Difficult and Enlightening Path

In one of the early scenes of the 1986 film *The Mission*, Rodrigo Mendoza finds himself in a deep depression. He had been a slave trader and a mercenary. Then, discovering that his fiancée had been romantically involved with his own brother, Rodrigo challenged the young man to a duel and killed him. Overwhelmed by guilt and shame, he now chooses to remain a recluse in his own home. His life, he feels, is forfeit.

The Jesuit priest, Father Gabriel, visits Rodrigo and challenges him to face his failures by taking up a penance that will allow him to truly repent and make amends. He helps him to see, by his sheer persistence and confidence in redemption, that there is always hope, even when the road is dark. Rodrigo agrees to accompany Father Gabriel and his Jesuit companions on a journey to the native peoples that he had formerly enslaved. His inward pursuit of selfishness and sin has been reoriented to a pilgrimage of repentance and an outward journey toward charity. For his penance he chooses to carry a heavy burden on his back, a bundle containing the armor and sword of his former life. The enormous bundle is awkward to carry and repeatedly forces him to the ground. At one point Father Gabriel decides that Rodrigo has carried the burden long enough, but Rodrigo stubbornly insists that the penance must endure still longer.

Suddenly the Jesuit company encounters a group of the natives and one of them, recognizing Rodrigo, lunges toward him with a knife. To the surprise and relief of all present, the native proceeds to cut the heavy pack away from Rodrigo. Realizing that he has been set free and also forgiven by the very people he had persecuted, he begins to weep uncontrollably. The natives cheer and laugh, causing Rodrigo to alternate between remorseful laughter and tears of joy. His sins had once crushed him and become a burden too heavy to bear, but now he has found release and a new beginning. Still, he will need to choose between the burden of his past and the new life to which he is being called.

✠ ✠ ✠

There are several possible meanings to the mystery of suffering. As we discussed in the previous chapter, experience teaches us all too well that we suffer as a consequence of selfishness and sin; because of our own poor decisions, or because of the sinful choices of those around us, we suffer. But even in situations when we cannot identify the source of suffering, we can all point to trials and difficulties that have taught us new insights and helped us to grow spiritually. While we would choose to avoid suffering, it can often help us to learn a great deal about ourselves and the world we live in. It may even bring a notion of meaning or purpose that we had not recognized before. This second meaning of suffering can be a challenging and even painful one for us to realize, however, so it requires further reflection. Let us begin by looking at Sacred Scripture.

Few persons in the Old Testament can match the mettle of the prophetess Judith. She was a beacon of light in the dark struggle against Israel's adversaries, the Assyrians. There are numerous paintings of Judith holding a sword in one hand and the head of Holofernes, general of the Assyrian army, in the other! When the elders of Israel begin to buckle at the threat of the Assyrians and are tempted to surrender the city of Bethulia, she speaks up and reminds them that God allows trials to strengthen us, not destroy us. She draws their attention to Abraham, Isaac, and Jacob, the great patriarchs who underwent tremendous difficulties in order to see God's plan bear fruit in their lives. "For he has not tried us with fire, as he did them," she exhorts, "to search their hearts, nor has he taken revenge upon us; but the Lord scourges those who draw near to him, in order to admonish them" (Judith 8:27).

Judith offers a valuable lesson for the elders, and for us. The brokenness and loss that we experience, even as a result of our own faults and weaknesses, can often be restored, healed, and purified in the furnace of affliction. Even the innocent who suffer frequently gain valuable insights about life and increase in virtue as a result of the trials they face. For example, a woman experiences discrimination in the workplace and goes on to make dignity and respect the hallmark of her professional life. A student athlete is unfairly cut from the team and then grows in the ability to include others and to show compassion. Suffering can and does teach a great deal of wisdom to those who are touched by it.

Not that we would ever want to seek out suffering, as if it were a value in and of itself. The story is told about Saint Teresa of Calcutta trying to console a dying patient undergoing a great deal of pain. She held the patient and said softly, "Whenever I experience pain in my life, I remember Jesus and try to see it as Him drawing close and kissing me." The patient seemed to understand, and beckoned the holy sister to come closer. Speaking into her ear, the woman said to the saint, "Could you please ask Jesus to stop kissing me?"

In his *Spiritual Canticle*, Saint John of the Cross reflects on how the road of suffering can often lead us through the caverns of the interior life, giving us access to the treasures found in Christ. "The soul," he writes, "cannot enter these caverns or reach these treasures if, as we said, she does not first pass over to the divine wisdom through the straits of exterior and interior suffering."[22] What Saint John of the Cross is advocating is not that we would willingly enter into the darkness as some kind of a test, but that we see the value in the suffering that comes to us despite our best efforts to avoid it. He describes access to these "caverns of Christ"[23] as a place of encounter, a space where God is present and begins to transform us in his love and mercy. We discover Christ there and grow in a deeper relationship with him.

---

22. Saint John of the Cross, *Spiritual Canticle*, in *The Collected Works of St. John of the Cross*, rev. ed., trans. Kieran Kavanaugh, O.C.D. and Otilio Rodriguez, O.C.D. (Washington, DC: ICS Publications, 1991), 616.

23. Saint John of the Cross, *Spiritual Canticle*, 616.

There are diamonds to be mined in this encounter with God, who meets us in our suffering. There is great potential for us to grow in virtue and in holiness as we see God restoring our souls and renewing our relationship with him. Suffering can indeed make us better.

On the other hand, we know that this is not the whole story. Suffering also has the potential to make us bitter. It can lead to anger, resentment, isolation, and despair. We do well to take account of the numerous souls in our world today who have ceased practicing their faith or broken off their relationship with God because of the confounding question of the cross. There is a tremendous risk, therefore, in a simplistic vision of suffering as classroom for wisdom and virtue. However valuable and instructive suffering may be, we once again conclude that there must be more to suffering than a lesson learned. Like the meaning of suffering as a consequence of sin, it rings true but is simply not enough. The suffering soul desires more than a classroom when it comes to the search for meaning. Thankfully, God, for his part, has much more to offer than a lesson. What he gives the soul searching for meaning is nothing less than his only begotten Son.

1. What is my reaction when I hear suffering described as a lesson to be learned?

2. Have I ever experienced a new beginning or healing after suffering and loss? Do I sense God's work of restoration in my own life at this time?

3. Have I ever learned a valuable lesson from suffering endured? How has suffering had an influence on shaping me as a person?

O GOD, ALMIGHTY FATHER, sin wearies us and sorrows weigh us down as we struggle to find our way to you. Often we struggle to find meaning and purpose and we seek to know your consoling presence in our lives. Help us to recognize you in the daily circumstances of life, teaching us that you have come into the world not to condemn, but to save and give new life. Give us the courage to walk in the freedom of the children of God. We ask this in the name of Jesus Christ, our Lord. Amen.

Chapter 6

Innocent Suffering

Seeking Balance in a Broken World

The morning of December 14, 2012, began like any other for the residents of Newtown, Connecticut. Families made ready for the day; parents shuffled off to work and children began a new day at school. But five minutes of unimaginable horror would shatter all sense of normalcy for the people of Newtown and for the nation. Between 9:35 and 9:40 a.m., a gunman forced himself into Sandy Hook Elementary School and took the lives of twenty first-grade children and six adults before turning the gun on himself. The word quickly forming in the hearts of so many grieving families on that dreadful morning would echo throughout the country: Why? The report issued a year later from the State Attorney tried to address it with honesty and accuracy:

"Unfortunately," the report stated, "that question may never be answered conclusively."[24]

✠ ✠ ✠

Suffering that comes as a result of our own sins is something that can be grasped. It is not an easy lesson, but we get it. To learn or discover some new insight and grow in wisdom through suffering is also within our reach. But the suffering of the innocent, and particularly something as senseless and devastating as the shooting at Sandy Hook, reduces every argument and explanation to silence.

Fyodor Dostoevsky's classic novel *The Brothers Karamazov* takes up the difficult question of innocent suffering with dramatic intensity. Ivan, the intellectually intense middle brother of the Karamazov clan, confronts young Alyosha, who has recently become a monk. Ivan describes several heartrending scenarios, one after the other, that leave his brother Alyosha perplexed and uneasy. Finally, Ivan comes to the heart of the matter: harmony.

The rational and scientific mind of Ivan ponders over cause and effect, transgression and justice. He comes to understand, and even accepts, that humanity must take responsibility for the injustice let loose on the earth. The human race had paradise, he concludes, and yet chose unhappiness instead.

---

24. "Report of the State's Attorney for the Judicial District of Danbury on the Shootings at Sandy Hook Elementary School [. . .]," November 25, 2013, https://portal.ct.gov/-/media/DCJ/SandyHook FinalReportpdf.pdf.

There is clearly a sense of just deserts at work here. But when it comes to suffering and sin, Ivan is unnerved by the proposal "that everything flows and finds its level," and with the possibility that "all must suffer to pay for the eternal harmony."[25] His own sin and suffering, along with that of humanity in general, might fit feasibly into this mysterious equation. But not the children. After Ivan details harrowing scenes of innocent suffering with cool precision, his demeanor suddenly changes. At the consideration of satisfying some eternal harmony by means of even one such innocent child, he defiantly declares, "I don't want harmony. From love for humanity I don't want it."[26]

Alyosha listens in silence until Ivan finally comes to his conclusion. Perhaps there may be a heaven, Ivan muses aloud, where the suffering of innocent children balances out transgressions and everything will make perfect sense in the end. If conceding to such a proposal is the cost of admission to heaven, though, Ivan will have none of it. "Too high a price is asked for harmony," he says, "it's beyond our means to pay so much to enter on it. And so I hasten to give back my entrance ticket, and if I am an honest man I am bound to give it back as soon as possible. And that I am doing. It's not God that I don't accept, Alyosha, only I most respectfully return Him the ticket."[27]

Ivan is not alone in his consternation before the suffering of the innocent. The question of God, in such cases, can make

25. Fyodor Dostoevsky, *The Brothers Karamazov*, trans. Constance Garnett (New York: Random House, 1996), 270–271.

26. Dostoevsky, *The Brothers Karamazov*, 272.

27. Dostoevsky, *The Brothers Karamazov*, 272.

the burden of suffering seem even more difficult. In his 1960 memoir, *Night,* author Elie Wiesel reflects on the horrors of the Holocaust, and it is precisely his faith in a loving God that comes into great conflict with the inhuman cruelty that he has personally experienced. When we encounter death or suffering and there seems to be no rational explanation or meaning at all, platitudes like "it was his time" or "everything happens for a reason" ring hollow. We want real answers, and we want to understand where God is in the midst of it all.

However definitive Ivan's rationale seems, it becomes clear in the novel that Dostoevsky is not yet finished with the question of suffering. Ivan's interpretation is not representative of the Christian tradition; God does not, in fact, require innocent children to suffer for the sake of humanity's transgressions. Nonetheless, Ivan's appeal to harmony and balance advances the question in an important direction. Something innately human longs for a return to paradise, to harmony and a change that would tip the world back in the right direction.

Jesus Christ has shifted the balance, in time and in eternity. The death and resurrection of Christ has completely unbalanced the way we understand sin and punishment, innocence and guilt, justice and mercy. Christ, the innocent one, suffers for the sake of the guilty, and with the intensity of a love that is freely given. He has come to take our punishment upon himself and to grant us pardon for our transgressions. In the place where justice was demanded because we had failed to follow the commandment of love, God has given us mercy through the blood of Christ. We have all been forgiven by God and this has the power to change the way we perceive the world around us. It also affects how willing we are to have compassion and mercy on others the way that God has had compassion and mercy on us. The risen Christ changes the balance between life and death itself. What had been a path with a definitive end—namely, death—has now become the beginning of new life. Since God became man and suffered and died for us, since Christ was raised from the dead, nothing will ever be the same again.

This very reality is where Dostoevsky weighs in on harmony and the suffering of the innocent. Immediately after Ivan declares that he will turn in his ticket for heaven, he sharply challenges the faith of young Alyosha. "Imagine that you are creating a fabric of human destiny with the object of making men happy in the end, giving them peace and rest at last, but that it was essential and inevitable to torture to death only one tiny creature . . . and to found that edifice on its unavenged tears, would you consent to be the architect on those conditions? Tell me, and tell the truth."[28]

Alyosha replies, in quiet resignation, that he would not consent to such a project. But then he shifts Ivan's own analogy ever so slightly. He moves away from the suffering of innocent children and instead focuses on the innocent suffering of Jesus Christ. He reminds Ivan, "There is a being and He can forgive everything, all and for all, because He gave His innocent blood for all and everything. You have forgotten Him, and on Him is built the edifice."[29]

The suffering and death of Jesus Christ does not erase the innocent suffering that we often witness in the broken world in which we live. It will not reverse the tragedies that have entered our lives so unexpectedly and left us numb with pain.

---

28. Dostoevsky, *The Brothers Karamazov*, 272.

29. Dostoevsky, *The Brothers Karamazov*, 273.

What his passion and death do signal, however, is that we are not alone when we suffer, and that God is not silent. He has spoken to us in the person of his Son, and he has ushered in a new beginning, a new hope for a life where there will be no more mourning and no more tears. The resurrection marks the first note in the song of salvation that will restore the harmony that God has desired from all eternity. We may not always hear that song clearly here in the world of human suffering, but with faith we can begin to tune into it even now.

1. Has the suffering of the innocent ever challenged my faith in a loving God?

2. How has the suffering of Christ changed me? How has it touched the world in which we live?

3. Has my faith changed the way that I consider and care for the innocent who suffer in the world each day?

O GOD, ALMIGHTY FATHER, the suffering in this world often wearies us, but the suffering of the innocent weighs on our souls. We long for answers and consolation, but especially for the peace and goodness that only you can give. Remember us when we encounter the evil of innocent suffering and help us to find our strength in you and to discover new life. We ask this in the name of Jesus Christ, our Lord. Amen.

CHAPTER 7

Light in the Darkness

Finding Love in an Unlikely Place

The year 1591 was a difficult one for Saint John of the Cross. Not that he would have considered it difficult, but the people who loved him most were distressed. After serving faithfully as prior of the Carmelites in Granada and then in Segovia, John had spoken out against some of the resolutions proposed by the vicar general at the extraordinary chapter in Madrid. When the vicar general was reelected, John was relieved of all responsibilities in the very order that he had helped reform.

Madre María de la Encarnación, a nun and spiritual daughter of the mystic saint, wrote to him in great agitation. She sought an explanation for the harm done to this man she loved so deeply. How could God allow this to happen? John's reply was a plea for her to trust in the Providence of God and remain firm in the faith that he is able to bring good even out

47

of suffering. "Think nothing else but that God ordains all," he wrote, "and where there is no love, put love, and you will draw out love."[30]

✠ ✠ ✠

Saint John of the Cross' counsel may at first seem like pious rubbish. If you look into a place and do not find love there, then you put love in that place; then when you look, you will find it. When God gives you lemons, you make lemonade, right? These words from the mystic and doctor of the Church, however, go much deeper than the surface level. What Saint John of the Cross describes is nothing less than the theology of the Incarnation.

When God looked at the world, he did not find the love that he wanted; the dream that he conceived for the human race was not as he had designed. There was a lack of love where love ought to be, and so God did something about it. He saw a world of great suffering, and in sending his only Son he altered that reality forever. If you look into a place and do not find love there, then you put love in that place; then when you look, you will find it. Jesus Christ is God's answer to a world awash in suffering.

"In order to perceive the true answer to the 'why' of suffering," insists Saint John Paul II, "we must look into the revelation of divine love, the ultimate source of meaning of everything that exists."[31] Truly God has done something

---

30. Saint John of the Cross, "Letter 26," in *The Collected Works of St. John of the Cross*, 760.

31. Saint John Paul II, *Salvifici Doloris*, no. 13.

unique in Christ when it comes to love and suffering. Those two realities are incongruent and normally mutually exclusive. In freely entering the passion and embracing the cross, Christ has placed the love he has for us and the suffering he endured to save us together in a way that is perplexing and demands our reflection. "God is love" (1 John 4:8), and love suffered for us all.

Not that this immediately answers all of the questions we have about suffering. The meaning of suffering, the Pope goes on to say, "always remains a mystery"[32] even if love does shine a strange new light into our darkness. To call something a mystery, however, does not mean that it remains unknown or obscure. God is a mystery. We will never fully know and understand, in this life, all there is to know about God. But we *can* know him, even love him; we can be loved *by* him. This can become, in fact, the source of hope and healing for the troubled heart. For Jesus Christ is "the light" that "shines in the darkness, and the darkness has not overcome it" (John 1:5).

We discover, in Christ, that we can still use our freedom and make difficult decisions even in the darkness of suffering. We are not helpless when we face the cross. His light allows us to see and helps us to navigate the perplexities and challenges that we face in life, and to choose intentionally how we will respond.

There is a beautiful scene in the first part of J. R. R. Tolkien's *The Lord of the Rings: The Fellowship of the Ring*. Having taken responsibility for the mysterious ring years before, only gradually does the hobbit Frodo begin to

---

32. Saint John Paul II, *Salvifici Doloris*, no. 13.

understand its perilous nature. However intriguing and even exciting the ring had been, he now sees that it could also wield a power that could destroy him. At the same time, he is able to see that his own sacrifice and careful choices could change the lives of those around him. It is not an impossible task for those who have courage, but who can be strong in the face of such danger? He unburdens himself in an intimate conversation with his friend Gandalf, lamenting that the ring has ever come to him. "I wish it need not have happened in my time," he cries.[33] Gandalf, with all the wisdom of his years and tremendous compassion, smiles gently at the little hobbit. "So do I," he says, "and so do all who live to see such times. But that is not for them to decide. All we have to decide is what to do with the time that is given us."[34] God does not expect us to solve all the problems that we face or to have all the answers to the difficulties of life. He does, however, give us the power to make the kind of decisions that Frodo ultimately makes in the midst of his difficult circumstances and that Saint John of the Cross counseled to Madre María de la Encarnación. We can always choose to bring something positive and constructive to the senselessness of suffering.

Even when we suffer, perhaps especially when we suffer, we are free. We can still make decisions, form opinions, listen to counsel, plot a course for the future. Within the scope of this field of human freedom, God has set before us particular virtues that act as guideposts, directing us onward toward the paths of peace. Three of the clearest and most powerful

---

33. J. R. R. Tolkien, *The Fellowship of the Ring* (New York: Houghton Mifflin Company, 1994), 50.

34. Tolkien, *The Fellowship of the Ring*, 50.

guideposts are the virtues of faith, hope, and charity. Will we follow these markers, asking for the grace to believe that God is present often in the very midst of our suffering and sorrow? Will we trust in his promises with hope-filled hearts, choosing freely the love being offered to us? Virtues are not earned through hard work and effort alone. Virtues are primarily a gift given, meaning that we must begin by asking for them and then by responding to the God who gives so generously and with so much love. In the words of Saint John of the Cross, "where there is no love, put love, and you will draw out love." We will find that love in the same place that he did.

1. Have I ever witnessed or experienced a time when love was freely added to a difficult situation? How did it change things?

2. How does Christ's incarnation touch my life personally and help me to see the fruits of God's love in my life?

3. What are some ways we can still use our freedom even when facing great challenges and suffering?

O GOD, ALMIGHTY FATHER, we are easily discouraged when we look into the world that you created and do not find love. Open our hearts to welcome you and strengthen our will to bring your love to these difficult places. Give us true freedom to make the choices and decisions that will allow us to be transformed, and help us to change the world we live in for good. We ask this in the name of Jesus Christ, our Lord. Amen.

CHAPTER 8

Christ the Redeemer

Overcoming the Ultimate Suffering

Several days had gone by since Martha and Mary had sent word to Jesus. Their brother, Lazarus, was very sick. As the illness worsened, the sisters had grown more anxious, until finally their brother had died. Now, they sat in silence in the house at Bethany. This place that had once been a beacon of life and love was now suffused with the pallor of death and sorrow.

Martha sensed movement near the doorway and heard murmuring. When she was told that Jesus was coming, her heart quickened for a moment and then the sadness washed over her like a wave. How she had longed for that announcement days ago, but now it was too late. Still, she rushed out to meet him. "Lord," she cried, "if you had been here, my brother would not have died" (John 11:21). It was hard for her to understand why her friend had come only now, but being in his presence somehow made her faith stronger. "And even now," she continued through tears, "I know that whatever you ask from God, God will give you" (John 11:22).

"Your brother will rise again," Jesus responded, but the words did not fully resonate in her heart, so overcome with grief (John 11:23). She struggled to know what to say and how to feel. Remembering well the many beautiful things he had taught her in the hours they had spent together, she reiterated the teaching of the resurrection that Jesus had spoken long before. Yes, of course he will rise again, on the last day.

After a brief pause, Jesus fixed his gaze upon her and spoke the words that would change her life forever. "I am the resurrection," he said with authority and love, "and the life" (John 11:25). It was not a *teaching* that had come to her in her suffering and pain, but the Teacher himself. He continued, ". . . he who believes in me, though he die, yet shall he live, and whoever lives and believes in me shall never die" (John 11:25–26).

For all of us, life will come to an end. It may happen silently, in our sleep at the end of many years. Or death may come earlier than we expected, accompanied by a physical struggle with difficult choices to be made. We do not know. Lazarus was miraculously raised to life by Jesus, but eventually he would leave this world. Along with his sisters, Martha and Mary, Lazarus would experience that final burial when his days on earth came to an end. What does the Christian faith have to say about this mysterious and daunting reality called death?

In Saint Luke's Gospel there is a heartrending scene that happens just outside the gates of a city called Nain. Jesus and his disciples are making their way into the city when they are confronted by a long procession of people moving in the opposite direction. These two separate groups halt, and then Luke gives us the context of that encounter: "A man who had died was being carried out, the only son of his mother, and she was a widow" (Luke 7:12). Next we read that Jesus had compassion on her; that was to be expected. But then he says to her, "Do not weep" (Luke 7:13). That was certainly not expected! Do not weep? She is a widow who has just lost her only son. What could have been going through the minds of those present, already weighed down by the sorrow of this tragic loss? Apparently this exchange was not witnessed by everyone, because the bearers continue to carry the body forward until Jesus does something else that no one could have anticipated: he ". . . touched the bier, and the bearers stood still. And he said, 'Young man, I say to you, arise'" (Luke 7:14). Suddenly the man sits up and begins to speak! This compelling Gospel passage shows Jesus reversing the direction of reality on several levels. He not only stops the inevitable advance of death, made present by that funeral procession, but changes even the existential reality of death itself. He speaks to the dead, and they come alive. Christ clearly has power over death. But in what sense?

Salvifici Doloris reflects on the often-quoted verse from Saint John's Gospel: "For God so loved the world that he gave his only Son, that whoever believes in him should not perish but have eternal life" (John 3:16). Here we find the story of salvation, marvelously packed into one powerful statement. Saint John Paul II describes salvation as "liberation from evil,"[35] freedom from the forces that seek to hold us bound not only in this life, but in the life to come. No longer are we considering suffering only as we find it in the temporal realm. The Gospel's hope for everlasting salvation exposes another, opposite reality: eternal loss, eternal suffering. *Salvifici Doloris* describes it as *"definitive suffering,"*[36] eternal separation from God. The gift that comes to us from the Father is Jesus Christ, our Redeemer, who seeks to heal our suffering and restore us to life eternal.

There will always be healing in this finite world and even second chances, like the one given to Lazarus or the widow's son at Nain. God came to dwell among us and promised that he would remain with us "to the close of the age" (Matthew 28:20). But whether or not we experience his healing touch here in this world and are given an entirely new lease on life, we are still finite beings. We face an ultimate reality that no miracle can alter. Jesus comes to save us from eternal suffering so that we might enter a life with him even now, a life that will eventually experience total liberation from all the sorrow and tears of this world. "Blessed are those who mourn," Jesus says, using the present tense, "for they shall be comforted" (Matthew 5:4). The beatitudes teach us that the blessed life is not just one that awaits us in the future, but that we can even now begin to taste the fruitful hope of eternal life. In a very real way, heaven floods into this present world when we seek to live the beatitudes and recognize that Christ is present to

---

35. Saint John Paul II, *Salvifici Doloris*, no. 14.

36. Saint John Paul II, *Salvifici Doloris*, no. 14.

us when we struggle. The suffering and death of Jesus Christ, and his ultimate resurrection from the dead, open a path of hope and healing right in the middle of this present reality. That path leads to an eternal life with him so that we will not perish but share in the fullness of salvation.

"Do you not know," asks Saint Paul, "that all of us who have been baptized into Christ Jesus were baptized into his death? We were buried therefore with him by baptism into death, so that as Christ was raised from the dead by the glory of the Father, we too might walk in newness of life" (Romans 6:3–4). Christ's suffering and death on the cross, and his rising from the dead, opens up an entirely new horizon for us who follow him. The Christ that we are buried with has already risen from the dead and longs to give us new life even now. Already we possess the joyful privilege to "walk in newness of life." That might not remove all our crosses in this life, but it can certainly change the way we understand them.

Toward the end of his life Saint Paul was imprisoned in Rome, having suffered much for the sake of the Gospel. He writes to Saint Timothy, "I am already on the point of being sacrificed; the time of my departure has come" (2 Timothy 4:6). Far from facing this moment with discouragement or fear, he concludes that he has "fought the good fight" (2 Timothy 4:7) and that "henceforth there is laid up for me the crown of righteousness" (2 Timothy 4:8). Never one to hoard for himself the abundant gifts of God, Saint Paul goes on to share that the same crown awaits all who devote themselves with patience to the revelation of Christ. We cannot know exactly how our lives will end, but we can know for certain the One who has gone before us and in whom we have been baptized. In fact, he is even now fashioning a crown for us, as he did for Saint Paul.

1. What is my initial reaction when I consider the reality of death? Where do I find Christ present in my thoughts about that transition from death to eternal life?

2. How might a growing relationship with Jesus, the Resurrection and the Life, change my present experience of suffering?

3. When I consider the Beatitude, "Blessed are those who mourn, for they shall be comforted," what does it stir up in my soul?

O GOD, ALMIGHTY FATHER, you sent Christ your Son to save us and set us free from eternal death and to give us everlasting life with you. Help us to experience even now the power of your love and the life of the resurrection. When our eyes are filled with tears of pain and sorrow, grant us the faith, hope, and love to know that you are near. We ask this in the name of Jesus Christ, our Lord. Amen.

CHAPTER 9

Gethsemane

Reclaiming the Garden

There is a beautiful story—more of a fairy tale or a parable—written by French authors Jerome and Jean Tharaud. The tale takes place on the night that Christ is born in Bethlehem. The shepherds and wise men have all come and gone, and suddenly an old woman appears in the doorway, dressed in rags. Mary is alarmed at the appearance of this haggard visitor, who is bent over as if weighed down by an impossible load. She makes her way toward the manger, each step seeming to take centuries to complete.

Mary is surprised to see that none of the animals are agitated by this uninvited guest. It is as if they knew she was coming all along. As the woman reaches the crib, she bends down toward the child, slowly producing something from beneath the fold of her wrinkled garments. Mary wonders what this mysterious gift might be. The old woman smiles knowingly at Mary as she departs, no longer bent over, her head now held high.

After the mysterious visitor has departed, Mary is able to see the curious gift that has been left with her son. It is an apple, small to behold but containing within it all of the sin of the world. It had been given to the child by Eve, who had come to visit the baby born for the redemption of all. She gave back what she had always regretted having taken, and paid homage to the child of her blood that had come to take away the sins of the world.

In the crib in Bethlehem lies the child that will save the world from sin. As early as the second century, Saint Irenaeus of Lyon wrote eloquently of Mary, the New Eve, who unties the knot of Eve's disobedience with her own magnificent "Fiat." But that can only take place because the fruit of her womb is the New Adam. It is his life that will flood the earth with hope and his death that will break open the gates of the netherworld. He is the Redeemer, the Savior, and the eternal Son of God.

The Son of God is a divine person, possessing two natures at the same time. Jesus Christ is both human and divine, true God and true man. The one who undergoes such devastating cruelty and endures the shame of crucifixion is God. In his human nature, he also suffers "as a man." What does that mean for us when we experience trials and suffering in this world?

The Letter to the Hebrews describes Christ as a High Priest fully capable of sympathizing with the weaknesses and struggles that we face each day, "one who in every respect has been tempted as we are, yet without sin" (Hebrews 4:15). This is an immediate consolation for us who yearn for a compassionate and understanding presence when we suffer. Jesus experienced exhaustion, thirst, and hunger; we understand that. He was rejected, isolated from those around him, and betrayed by his own friends; we have also been there. But what about sin? If he was without sin, can we truly say that he is like us?

Cardinal Albert Vanhoye, in his theological reflection on the High Priesthood of Christ, confronts this challenging question. Can Christ share completely in solidarity with suffering humanity if he has not experienced sin? Vanhoye notes that sin "is always an act of egoism, in one form or another, which creates division and a lack of solidarity."[37] Sin has nothing to do with solidarity. In fact, sin is what destroys solidarity and communion. Christ has come to restore those very things, and he does so by completely uniting himself to us. Nowhere is that restoration more evident or more powerful than his passion. It is specifically in the sacred space of human freedom that Jesus Christ redeems us and restores all things.

It is fallen humanity that has violated that sacred space and brought into it everything profane. Sin is not created by God; that is our contribution. We have brought into the world what God never intended because, having sinned, we freely chose to reject the God who made us. By freely choosing to enter this same space that we have rendered profane, Jesus

---

37. Cardinal Albert Vanhoye, *Christ Our High Priest* (Herefordshire: Gracewing, 2010), 51.

Christ alone as God has the power to restore it to its original orientation.

In a remarkable summary of the reality of redemptive suffering, Saint John Paul II writes, "In his suffering, sins are cancelled out precisely because he alone as the only-begotten Son could take them upon himself." He alone could "accept them *with that love for the Father which overcomes* the evil of every sin; in a certain sense he annihilates this evil in the spiritual space of the relationship between God and humanity, and fills this space with good."[38]

This happens in the most dramatic way in the Garden of Gethsemane. So very different from the Garden of Eden, that plush and fertile place where Adam and Eve first chose selfishness over generosity—"My will be done, God, not thine"—Gethsemane brings us face to face with the darkness of sin. Christ kneels in that hostile place where the Father of Lies will attack him and seek to undermine his very mission and purpose. Because he shares fully in our humanity, he does not want to die. He would have it otherwise, but he has not come to do his own will. "My Father," he prays in that agonizing moment, "if it be possible, let this cup pass from me; nevertheless, not as I will, but as thou wilt" (Matthew 26:39).

In his passion, Christ undoes the ancient curse of sin by taking our own willful disobedience upon himself. His loving obedience to the Father lived out through his suffering on the Cross ushers in our redemption and the hope for a new beginning. Because he shares completely in our human nature and because we are fully united to him in Baptism, we now possess the power to kneel with him in that same garden and

---

38. Saint John Paul II, *Salvifici Doloris*, no. 17. Italics in original.

participate in our own way in that sacred space. The American poet Ella Wheeler Wilcox muses:

> Down shadowy lanes, across strange streams
> Bridged over by our broken dreams;
> Behind the misty caps of years,
> Beyond the great salt font of tears,
> The garden lies. Strive as you may,
> You cannot miss it on your way.
> All paths that have been or shall be,
> Pass somewhere through Gethsemane.
>
> All those who journey, soon or late,
> Must pass within the garden's gate;
> Must kneel alone in darkness there,
> And battle with some fierce despair.
> God pity those who cannot say,
> "Not mine but thine," who only pray,
> "Let this cup pass," and cannot see
> The purpose of Gethsemane.[39]

In a silent crib in Bethlehem, a child waits in the cool of the evening as angels line the sky. His tiny body will one day lie prostrate in Gethsemane as an offering of love to the Father's will, but tonight he is content to curl up in the warmth of the manger. A Virgin, expert at untying knots and interceding for the Sons and Daughters of Adam, lifts her kind, soft eyes and glances your way. Those eyes, almost too beautiful to look at, beckon and invite in a way that strengthens freedom and courage. "Do you have something for the child?" they seem to say. He is ready to receive you.

---

39. Ella Wheeler Wilcox, "Gethsemane," in *Poems of Ella Wheeler Wilcox* (Edinburgh: W. P. Nimmo, Hat and Mitchell, 1889), 168.

1. Where, in the sufferings of Christ, can I identify some of my own experiences of suffering?

2. How might God be calling me to kneel in Gethsemane and unite my will more completely to his will?

3. Are there any sins or failings in my life that I would like to give to God as I seek his healing forgiveness and grace?

O GOD, ALMIGHTY FATHER, you sent your only-begotten Son to be born in Bethlehem to save us from our sins. We are often weighed down by the burdens that we carry and seek the grace of redemption. Come to us in our weakness and teach us once again to use our freedom for our good and your glory. Show us the way to unite our will to yours. We ask this in the name of Jesus Christ, our Lord. Amen.

CHAPTER 10

Sign of the Cross

Suffering Redeemed

The warmth of the autumn sun spreads generously across the Assisi hillside, bathing everything it touches in golden splendor. It is the year 1205, and the natural beauty of the Umbrian countryside holds a particular attraction for a young man named Francis. He walks across the open land without any itinerary, but not without purpose. "Has our city always been this captivating?" He asks the question aloud, to no one but the meadow and a row of olive trees. Smiling, he gently chides himself for having been so blind for too long. Each new step seems to take him farther along into this new-found awareness of the created world and of God. He has never felt more alive.

Spying an old, abandoned church nestled in the hillside, he frowns for a moment and then makes his way toward it.

He is drawn to the place, like a thirsty hart seeking a cool stream in the wilderness. He enters through the gaping vestibule; its doors have long ago been sacrificed for firewood or some other base purpose. The walls of San Damiano are crumbling as shafts of sunlight spill in through the apertures where large stones had once been. Francis' attention becomes fixed on a massive wooden cross in the sanctuary, undisturbed except for the heavy dust of many years. He kneels before it, tears streaming down his face and dotting the dirt floor beneath him. "For me," he whispers to no one. "For me." The large eyes of Christ on the cross are warm and inviting. They seem to silently reply to the little poor man: *Yes, for you.* Francis remains there for a long time, practicing the ancient art of listening to God in the silence.

Then, suddenly, he hears a voice. It is not an interior intuition but an audible sound, something that he listens to, as Saint Bonaventure will later describe, "with the ears of his body." It is coming from the cross itself. Three times it addresses him in the same words: "Francis, go, repair my house, which, as you see, is falling completely to ruin."[40] Looking around at the dilapidated church, he is moved with sorrow and a firm resolve. Like a man who suddenly discovers his vocation, his very calling in life, he begins to repair that ruined edifice. He is humbled by the great honor that has been entrusted to him. He is ready to give his life to make the Church of San Damiano beautiful and sacred once again. He is yet unaware that the command refers to the

---

40. Thomas of Celano, *Saint Francis of Assisi*, trans. Placid Hermann (Chicago: Franciscan Herald Press, 1988), 144.

entire Catholic Church throughout the world, and that this seemingly impossible task will already begin to take place in his lifetime.

The miracle of the San Damiano Cross is widely known and is foundational for the life of Saint Francis of Assisi. It is not, however, the first time that the cross has communicated something deeply personal to the followers of Christ crucified. Saint Paul had a profound affection for it, declaring, "Far be it from me to glory except in the cross of our Lord Jesus Christ, by which the world has been crucified to me, and I to the world" (Galatians 6:14). In the early fourth century, the Emperor Constantine had a vision of the cross before his victory at the Milvian Bridge and believed that this was the sign through which he had conquered. It became the impetus for his conversion to the Christian faith. The discovery of the True Cross is attributed to the mother of Constantine, Saint Helena, who went to the Holy Land in search of this great relic and brought it back to Rome. From this point forward devotion to the cross built momentum.

There is a manuscript dating back to the late tenth century that contains a poem, "The Dream of the Rood." It tells of a vision in which the cross relates firsthand the dramatic events of the suffering and death of Christ. *Rood* is an Old English word for the screen that separated the sanctuary from the nave, or main body, of the church. In the Middle Ages, the cross was often fastened to the rood screen; over time the word became synonymous with the cross itself. An elaborate reliquary in the Brussels' Cathedral of St. Michael and St.

Gudula holds a relic of the True Cross. Engraved on that silver reliquary are two lines from "The Dream of the Rood":

> Rood is my name; once, trembling, covered with blood,
>   I bore the great King.[41]

In that poem the Rood goes on to speak of its shameful origins. It was not hewed from the handsome stock used by craftsmen, but roughly assembled as an instrument for torture. "They made me a hoist for wrongdoers," says the Rood, and it is in this context that it encounters "mankind's brave King."[42] He did not come reluctantly, but willingly climbed upon the Rood, eager to redeem fallen humanity. In that fateful moment, the Rood comes to share the same fate as the Lord, blow for blow:

> They drove me through with dark nails:
>   on me are the deep wounds manifest,
> wide-mouthed hate-dents.
>   I durst not harm any of them.
> How they mocked at us both!
>   I was all moist with blood
> sprung from the man's side
>   after He sent forth His soul.[43]

Devastated, the Rood then witnesses the deposition of Christ. It signals that it is not alone in that sorrow, as "all creation wept."[44] It watches helplessly as the faithful disciples of

---

41. "The Dream of the Rood," in *The First Poems in English*, trans. Michael Alexander (London: Penguin Books, 2008), 31.

42. "The Dream of the Rood," 38.

43. "The Dream of the Rood," 39.

44. "The Dream of the Rood," 39.

Christ take his body and place it in the tomb. Sharing a similar fate, the Rood is also leveled to the ground and buried beneath the earth. At this point, a strange and unexpected transformation begins. The friends of Christ come in search of the Rood; they soon adorn the cross with silver, gold, and precious stones. It has changed significantly from an instrument of torture to the "tree of glory."[45] Having fully embraced its newfound identity, it declares openly to the dreamer, "The time has now come that men on earth, and all this marvelous creation, shall honor me far and wide and address themselves in prayer to this sign."[46]

The reluctance of the Rood at its initial encounter with the suffering Christ is indicative of our own experience of the cross. We are often surprised by the suffering that comes into our lives, believing that we are made for a more noble purpose. The journey of the Rood is instructive as it traces the trajectory of shame and sorrow but ultimately grows into an intimacy with the crucified One. The end of that encounter is glory, shared now with the risen Christ. The first experience of suffering is always a negative one, but it can also open us to an intimate encounter with Christ. He lovingly calls to us in the midst of our own sufferings and welcomes us to join him in that noble struggle that will end in redemption and new life.

In one of the more striking declarations of *Salvifici Doloris*, Saint John Paul II insists, "In the cross of Christ not only is the Redemption accomplished through suffering, but also human suffering itself has been redeemed."[47] It is not the case

---

45. "The Dream of the Rood," 40.

46. "The Dream of the Rood," 40.

47. Saint John Paul II, *Salvifici Doloris*, no. 19.

that there could be value or meaning in suffering for its own sake; it is simply that Christ has done something unprecedented in the long history of human suffering. He has entered that "spiritual space"[48] of the relationship between God and man in the most unseemly of moments. Christ has mounted the hill of Calvary and placed the offering of love within human suffering. In his remarkable generosity he has radically changed even suffering itself. He plants the seeds for the annihilation of that evil and creates the good of the redemption.

In a homily for the Feast of the Apostles Saint Peter and Saint Paul, Pope Benedict XVI explains how Christ's sacrifice on the cross attacks the evil of sin with this same offering of love. "In his passion," he says, "he went deep down into the sordid darkness of our sins. He went down into the night of our guilt, for only thus can it be transformed."[49] The darkness of sin must yield to the light of God's love and the power of his forgiveness. As the *Catechism of the Catholic Church* explains, "The obedience of Jesus has transformed the curse of death into a blessing."[50] Sin and suffering can both remain what they always were: empty, vile, destructive, and evil. But with the offering of Jesus Christ on the cross they can also become instrumental in the reawakening of our spiritual lives. Awareness of all that Christ has accomplished for love opens our hearts to the mercy and grace that he willingly shares with us for the renewal of our lives. Suffering can also make us

---

48. Saint John Paul II, *Salvifici Doloris*, no. 17.

49. Pope Benedict XVI, "Holy Mass for the Imposition of the Sacred Pallium on Metropolitan Archbishops," June 29, 2011, https://www.vatican.va/content/benedict-xvi/en/homilies/2011/documents/hf_ben-xvi_hom_20110629_pallio.html.

50. *Catechism of the Catholic Church*, no. 1009.

aware of the presence of God and open the way for that same transformation.

The Letter to the Hebrews offers a surprising and lucid commentary on the passion of Christ. It states: "In the days of his flesh, Jesus offered up prayers and supplications, with loud cries and tears, to him who was able to save him from death, and he was heard for his godly fear. Although he was a Son, he learned obedience through what he suffered; and being made perfect he became the source of eternal salvation to all who obey him" (Hebrews 5:7–9). It seems odd to consider that Christ learned obedience. Cardinal Albert Vanhoye writes that Christ himself "did not need this suffering education," but that it is something he willingly undergoes for our sake.[51] Noting the superabundant obedience of Christ, Vanhoye indicates that this obedience is now made available for us. "Christ," he explains, "is able to communicate to us his profound docility to God."[52] The cross of Christ—with all of its prayers and supplications, loud cries and tears—has become the path to glory.

The conclusion of "The Dream of the Rood" offers a universal exhortation regarding the final judgment, when Christ will come again. Everyone, says the Rood, will have to give an account of their lives, and many will be left speechless. "Yet no one there will be left afraid," it affirms, "who has borne in his bosom the best of signs. But every soul on earth who intends to dwell with the Lord shall come to the Kingdom through the Rood."[53]

51. Vanhoye, *Christ Our High Priest*, 61.

52. Vanhoye, *Christ Our High Priest*, 61.

53. "The Dream of the Rood," 41.

1. Has suffering ever surprised me or caught me off guard? When I have experienced the cross, what has my initial reaction been?

2. What is my reaction when I hear that my suffering could become a sharing in the suffering of Jesus Christ? Does this possibility seem daunting or overwhelming, or comforting?

3. How might my suffering, joined with Christ, become an occasion for the reawakening of my spiritual life? What could pose an obstacle to this reawakening?

O GOD, ALMIGHTY FATHER, your Son willingly embraced the cross to save us and to bring us new life. Our own experience of the cross is often difficult and even overwhelming. Help us to recognize Jesus in the midst of our suffering, and to know that he is with us. Grant us the courage and the generosity to unite ourselves to him and to participate in the redemption that transforms the world. We ask this in the name of Jesus Christ, our Lord. Amen.

CHAPTER 11

Eucharistic Suffering

Christ, the Good and Loving Pelican

The majestic pelican glides toward her nest after atten-tively patrolling the coastal waters. She carefully lands on its edge as her nestlings crowd around her. Without warning she thrusts her enormous beak into her breast, again and again. Blood and flesh appear as red blotches on her white and brown feathers. Methodically, she begins to feed her young.

The pelican is a symbol for Christ that goes all the way back to the second century. Early Christians would see that magnificent bird apparently piercing her own breast with her beak and then proceeding to feed her young chicks. It was moving to witness the pain and sacrifice that the pelican was willing to undergo in order to feed and care for her young. In actuality, the pelican was clearing her beak of the small fish she had caught and pressing them against her breast as she went to pass them on to her nestlings. The blood manifest on the pelican's breast was from the fish, not the pelican. The Christian faithful, nonetheless, saw in this an image of Jesus Christ, who allows himself to be pierced so that he can feed us with his own Body and Blood in the Eucharist.

✣ ✣ ✣

If you visit many of the great Gothic cathedrals or magnificent basilicas throughout the world, in splendid marble altar pieces and luminous stained glass arrangements you will see images of the pelican. Saint Thomas Aquinas, in his breathtaking Eucharistic hymn *Adóro Te Devóte*, writes eloquently of Christ, the good and loving pelican:

Pie pellicane Iesu Domine
Me immundum munda tuo sanguine
Cuius una stilla salvum facere
Totum mundum quit ab omni scelere.[54]

A pitying pelican, dear Jesus, be;
Save by the blood thou sheddest on the tree,
My starving soul,—thy precious blood, whereof,
One drop from every crime the world can free.[55]

In the Cathedral of St. Michael and St. Gudula, there is a side sanctuary called Our Lady's Chapel. It is dedicated to

---

54. Rev. Randy Soto, ed., *Manual of Prayers*, 3rd ed. (Downers Grove, IL: Midwest Theological Forum, 2021), 376.

55. Daniel Joseph Donahoe, *Early Christian Hymns: Translations of the Verses of the Most Notable Latin Writers of the Early and Middle Ages* (New York: Grafton Press, 1908), 189–190.

Our Lady of Deliverance, and there is an impressive altar there held up by two enormous sculpted pelicans. One of them is piercing its side with its beak, while the other stretches its head up toward the altar. Two generous outstretched wings support the altar above. The symbol is clear: Christ allows himself to be pierced and wounded on the altar of the cross so that he can feed us with his Body and Blood in the Eucharist.

Chapter 14 of the Gospel of Saint Matthew offers a poignant expression of Jesus, the good and holy pelican. Saint Matthew tells us that Jesus has just learned of the death of Saint John the Baptist. Remember, John was his cousin; Jesus obviously loved him a great deal. Having heard of John's execution, Jesus did the most fitting and expected thing perhaps any one of us would have done: "he withdrew from there in a boat to a lonely place apart" (Matthew 14:13). He wanted to be alone with God.

Suddenly, though, the crowds who have anticipated his arrival surround him as he disembarks. There will be neither silence nor solitude for Christ in this grief-filled hour. But how remarkable, the response of our Lord! He does not become frustrated or flustered; he complains not in the least. Instead, we are told that "he had compassion on them, and healed their sick" (Matthew 14:14). In the midst of his own personal loss and from the depths of his vulnerability, he loves them and feeds them. Still fresh from the experience of the death of the Baptist, he who is still wounded reaches into the depths of himself and teaches them. He preaches the Gospel of the Kingdom of God to them, and they hear him gladly, all day long.

As the sun begins to set, the disciples size up the situation and recommend that the Master dismiss the crowds. There are thousands of people, and they have no food. "They need not go away," Jesus responds; "you give them something to eat" (Matthew 14:16). The disciples are astounded. Nonetheless, they bring to him the simple offering of five loaves and two fish. Jesus, the good and loving pelican, brings the loaves to his breast and breaks them; he gives thanks to God for these gifts and then distributes them to his disciples, who in turn give them to the hungry crowd.

The great miracle of the Feeding of the Five Thousand, of course, is a foreshadowing of the miracle of our Lord's Body and Blood in the Eucharist. On the night before he suffers and dies on the cross, Jesus takes bread, exactly as he does here, and he breaks the bread, giving thanks to God and saying, "This is my body which is given for you. Do this in remembrance of me" (Luke 22:19). He distributes his Body and his Blood to them at that sacred meal and all are nourished. He who was pierced and wounded on the cross, this good and holy pelican, feeds us with himself in the bread and wine that becomes his Body and Blood for the life of the world.

The Eucharist is the greatest Gift we could ever receive on this earth because it is the very Gift of God himself in love for us. But that Gift only comes to us through the suffering and death of Jesus Christ. The Lord's great work of redeeming the world is not something he holds on to but a gift that he most willingly shares. He feeds us, forgives us, heals us, and sends us forth as wounded healers.

During my first winter as a seminarian in Europe, I was able to attend Christmas Mass at Wawel Cathedral in Krakow, Poland. The church was completely filled, leaving many of the faithful standing in the aisle. When it came time for communion, the people all knelt right where they were, and the priest walked up and down the aisle distributing the Eucharist to each one. One woman was kneeling next to her son, but the boy was so small that the priest missed him and, after giving communion to the mother, he simply moved on. The woman quickly raised up her young charge and moved him farther up the line, having him kneel down a second time. The priest missed him again! By this time, those who had already received communion were drawn to this little drama and people were trying to make space for the boy so that he could finally receive the Blessed Sacrament. The mother, undaunted, brought him farther down the line for a third try. When the priest finally recognized the young communicant and gave him the Body of Christ, there were audible sighs of relief. That woman was going to stop at nothing to make sure her son received the Lord on Christmas morning. There is something of that maternal love in each one of us, and there are many souls that depend upon that persistent care that we can bring to those in need.

Suffering can often leave us helpless and hungry for the healing that Christ alone can give. The pierced One feeds us with himself and constantly reminds us that we are not alone. This consolation can become our motivation for reaching out to others in their suffering and being a source of strength for those who buckle beneath the burden of the cross. Through our prayers, and perhaps even through our suffering, we seek to bring others closer to our Eucharistic Lord. For it is his Body alone which heals and saves us, and his Blood,

"whereof, One drop from every crime the world can free."[56]

1. In what way does suffering make me needy or hungry for the consolation of God?

---

56. Donahoe, *Early Christian Hymns*, 190.

2. What is my reaction when I imagine Jesus as needy and suffering even as he is feeding the crowds and teaching them?

3. How might God be calling me to be a source of strength or help for others who are suffering?

O GOD, ALMIGHTY FATHER, we stand in awe of your love and generosity in giving us your only-begotten Son as food and sustenance. From the midst of his own suffering, Christ fills us with life and gives us strength. Help us to be renewed in the Eucharist and to become wounded healers in our world. We ask this in the name of Jesus Christ, our Lord. Amen.

PART II

How We Suffer

CHAPTER 12

The "Fortunate" One

The Path to Freedom

She had been born in Darfur in 1869. It was the year of the flood when the Blue Nile and the White Nile overflowed their banks. In fact, her entire life was one swept up into a current of uncertainty, violence, and abuse. Today the river of tears brings her to Sudan's capital city, Khartoum. The men are bargaining a few feet away, carrying out their exchange amid the din of the nearby marketplace. She sits calmly, not because she is indifferent but because this is all she knows. The exchange is complete within a few minutes; the merchant pays the negotiated price, and the Italian Consulate now has a new servant. What she will be asked to do she does not know. She only hopes that this new master will not be worse than the last one.

Closing her eyes, she drifts back to the terrifying day when it all began. She had been nine years old. Armed men had invaded her family's property and dragged her away by force. Not long after, she went through the exchange for the first time. Angry, serious-minded men were arguing, arbitrating. Everything then became quiet; one man grunted and there were sighs and small talk as the tension eased. One of her captors shouted something in her direction, then began dragging her to the other men. "Your name!" he yelled, but she was too afraid to even understand what he meant. "What is your name?" She was frozen in fear. Turning back to the purchasers, the man shrugged and then paused, his rough face a silent mask of reflection. A smile began to form, though it never reached his eyes. "Bakhita," he said: the Arabic word for fortunate. "This one is Bakhita." And all the men began to laugh.

Bakhita opens her eyes, back in Khartoum. The Italian merchant finishes counting out the payment. At his direction she is on her way. Although she has been through this experience five times, she cannot escape the feeling that this one is different. With an unconscious straightening of her shoulders and a deep breath, she summons that inner strength of which she possesses no small amount. The warm sun is rising over Sudan's Blue Nile River, and for a moment Bakhita feels almost like it is calling to her. Her eyes squint as she glances at the horizon before slowly letting her head fall back down.

What Bakhita could not have known, of course, was that another exchange had already taken place long ago. There had already been a price paid for her freedom, and she was awaited by the one who had loved her before she was even born—not another slave master, but the God who emptied himself to become a servant to all. She could have never imagined that in a few short years she would be baptized Josephine Bakhita, a daughter of God, or that she would one day be the patron saint of Sudan and victims of human trafficking.

Pope Francis has addressed the subject of human trafficking many times. He has referred to this bitter reality as an "abhorrent plague"[57] and an "open wound on the body of contemporary society."[58] It is a pandemic, an illness infecting countless souls through the exploitation of the body. The numbers are staggering. International organizations estimate that millions of people worldwide are victims of human trafficking and forced labor—numbers that only seem to be rising from year to year. The shadow of human trafficking has fallen on every part of the world and is found in a variety of abuses, including slave labor, child soldiers, and the trafficking of organs. This multi-billion dollar industry is growing at an alarming rate, and an astounding two-thirds of that business consists of sexual exploitation.[59]

Human trafficking is not a form of suffering that can ever be viewed in a positive light. Pope Francis has consistently signaled that human trafficking is an evil that should be opposed and resisted on every level, and by all possible means.

---

57. Pope Francis, "Angelus," The Holy See, July 30, 2017. https://www.vatican.va/content/francesco/en/angelus/2017/documents/papa-francesco_angelus_20170730.html.

58. Pope Francis, "Address to Participants in the International Conference on Combatting Human Trafficking," The Holy See, April 10, 2014,https://www.vatican.va/content/francesco/en/speeches/2014/april/documents/papa-francesco_20140410_tratta-persone-umane.html.

59. International Labor Organization, "2022 Global Estimates of Modern Slavery,"https://www.ilo.org/wcmsp5/groups/public/---ed_norm/---ipec/documents/publication/wcms_854733.pdf.

In the homily for the Mass of Canonization of Saint Josephine Bakhita, patron saint of victims of human trafficking, Saint John Paul II noted, "In today's world, countless women continue to be victimized, even in developed and modern societies. In Josephine Bakhita we find *a shining advocate of genuine emancipation.* The history of her life inspires not passive acceptance but the firm resolve to work to free girls and women from oppression and violence, and to return them to their dignity in the full exercise of their rights."[60]

Those who have never experienced the horrors of human slavery can only imagine that enormous fight for freedom. However, we can all identify with the need to be free of the constraints that keep us bound when we suffer. "For freedom Christ has set us free" (Galatians 5:1), Saint Paul admonishes us. He who had spent a great deal of his life as a captive explains the nature of the Christian faith: to be completely the men and women we are called to be in Christ despite the circumstances that would tell us otherwise.

To acknowledge that Jesus Christ has redeemed us through his generous gift of self on the cross is at the heart of the saving message of the Gospel. Recognizing that even suffering itself has been redeemed at Calvary has the power to open up sources of hope and healing never before imaginable. Nonetheless, a value or meaning cannot automatically be assigned to suffering itself. Suffering is always an experience of evil,[61] and as such it should be met with resistance.

---

60. "Homily of John Paul II" The Holy See, October 1, 2000, https://www.vatican.va/content/john-paul-ii/en/homilies/2000/documents/hf_jp-ii_hom_20001001_canonization.html.

61. Saint John Paul II, *Salvifci Doloris*, no. 7.

German Lutheran theologian Dorothy Söelle was one of the more strident voices opposing a facile acceptance to suffering, particularly when embraced under the guise of faith. Söelle considered passive acceptance of suffering by individuals to be a form of masochism. On a societal level, she insisted that "for centuries the cult of suffering has been shamelessly exploited to justify injustice and oppression."[62]

With regard to modern slavery, it is a well-established fact that traffickers subtly manipulate their victims to keep them psychologically chained through shame and despair. Globally, it is allowed to continue not only because of the malice of the traffickers or the reality of the demand, but also because of a lack of awareness and an unwillingness to eradicate it from the structures of society. Pope Francis has called for a response comparable to the reality of trafficking itself, supplanting organized networks of crime with organized networks for good. He has implored the world "not to become accomplices to this evil, not to turn away from the sufferings of our brothers and sisters, our fellow human beings, who are deprived of their freedom and dignity. Instead, may we have the courage to touch the suffering flesh of Christ."[63] We are called to resist human suffering and evil, but to accept, love, and welcome those who suffer as if the victim of human trafficking were Christ himself.

---

62. Dorothy Söelle, *Suffering* (Philadelphia: Fortress Press, 1975), 103.

63. Pope Francis, "World Day of Prayer for Peace," The Holy See, January 1, 2015, https://www.vatican.va/content/francesco/en/messages/peace/documents/papa-francesco_20141208_messaggio-xlviii-giornata-mondiale-pace-2015.html.

This is true not just for victims of human trafficking, but for everyone who endures suffering. In Sacred Scripture, Christ clearly confronted his own suffering with resistance at Gethsemane, asking three times that the chalice of affliction be removed. Likewise, Saint Paul pleaded three times that the Lord remove his "thorn in the flesh,"[64] only to receive the mysterious and promising reply, "My grace is sufficient for you, for my power is made perfect in weakness" (2 Corinthians 12:9). There is a clear and challenging pattern here of resistance, but also of acceptance. Christ wanted the chalice of suffering to be taken away, but within a day he had consummated the work of our redemption. Saint Paul's thorn in the flesh remains, but it does not prevent him from giving himself generously to the work of the Gospel.

Nowhere in the Gospel, however, do we find a passive acceptance of suffering or any sense that the cross has value apart from Christ's redeeming love. Jesus teaches us to turn the other cheek when we are struck (see Matthew 5:39), but he never invites us to be passive victims. In the depths of our hearts, we are always called to acknowledge our human dignity. We are worth all of Christ's blood. It is not suffering that redeems the world; it is the offering of love on the cross that saves us.

This truth forms an essential foundation for the theology of redemptive suffering. Without it, there is always a risk of isolating the suffering person who is perhaps already

---

64. Biblical commentaries speculate on what exactly this "thorn in the flesh" was for Paul, whether some physical ailment, psychological burden or perhaps even a struggle with a particular sin. For our purposes, it is clear enough that it was an affliction and he wanted it removed.

overwhelmed by the weight of the cross. If there is some way to avoid the evil of suffering, then it is well within the bounds of reason and faith to do so. If we find ourselves in a position to alleviate the pain, distress, and hardship of others, then we have an obligation to be an active force for change.

Saint Maximilian Kolbe, for example, lived an austere life and willingly united his sufferings to Christ as a prisoner at Auschwitz, yet it was his compassion for a condemned prisoner that led him to take the man's place and offer his life in love. He saw an opportunity to spare another soul from great suffering, and he gave everything to make that happen. Saint Teresa of Calcutta was a woman who embraced suffering all her life, yet she was a catalyst for change and a force for the alleviation of the suffering poor.

We see from these examples and many others that redemptive suffering does not mean being passive, accepting all injustice and evil in the circumstances we face. Resistance in the face of the cross is perfectly consonant with a mature and faithful spiritual life. Yet, when the cross remains, we are reminded by Sacred Scripture and the lives of the saints that we are not alone. There exists "so great a cloud of witnesses" (Hebrews 12:1), cheering us on and offering support, strength, and prayers. We fix our eyes on Jesus and seek to remain open to the examples of the saints who teach us, in every age, how to carry the cross and discover hope.

Bakhita began her work as a servant to the Italian consul, Callisto Legnani, but the political turmoil of that time would force him to retreat back to Italy as the Mahdists were set to take over Sudan. Bakhita pleaded that Legnani take her with him. Once in Italy, she began to discover a totally new way of life. One of her tasks was to accompany a young girl to the school that was run by the Congregation of the Canossian

Sisters. Both in the place where she lived and among these sisters who were so dedicated and fervent, Bakhita began to experience something she had not encountered since the day she was kidnapped. Her heart was being reawakened to the love she had felt as a child, and the community of sisters were helping her to understand that this mysterious love was God himself.

As she had done since childhood, Bakhita took in the magnificent night sky and the magnetic attraction of nature. She did so with the overwhelming sense that she was not alone in the world. She would later comment, "Seeing the sun, moon and the stars, I said to myself: Who could be Master of these beautiful things? And I felt a great desire to see him, to know him, and to pay homage."[65] Not long after, she began instruction in the Catholic faith with the Canossian Sisters.

This whole new experience was suddenly threatened as the Italian family she was serving intended to bring her back to Sudan. She resisted. After a long and dramatic court battle, she was finally given her freedom. In fact, she had already been legally free, since slavery was illegal in Sudan at the time of her kidnapping. More importantly, she had always been called to inherit "the glorious liberty of the children of God" (Romans 8:21).

Following the natural direction of her heart, now moved by grace, she completed her instruction in the Catholic faith. In 1890 she was baptized, confirmed, and received her First Communion from the Patriarch of Venice. When she was

---

65. "Josephine Bakhita (1869–1947)," The Holy See, https://www. vatican.va/news_services/liturgy/saints/ns_lit_doc_20001001_ giuseppina-bakhita_en.html.

told that she could choose any name she wanted in Baptism, finally free to dispense with the cruel name assigned by her captors, she refused. She had become a daughter of God, and so considered herself most fortunate. Having at the same time a deep devotion to Saint Joseph, she chose the name Josephine Bakhita.

In 1896 she professed vows in the Congregation of the Canossian Sisters, serving joyfully in that community for the next fifty years until the Lord called her home. Considering her life and all that she had experienced, she once concluded, "I am definitively loved and whatever happens to me—I am awaited by this love. And so my life is good."[66]

1. Have I ever been tempted to remain passive in the midst of the struggles and suffering that I have experienced?

2. What are some of the ways I can exercise my freedom even if the circumstances of my life do not change the way I would like them to?

3. How could my choices make a positive impact on those around me who are suffering?

O GOD, ALMIGHTY FATHER, when we find ourselves bound and constrained by the difficulties that we face, remind us that you created us to be free. Come into our hearts and help us to

---

66. Pope Benedict XVI, *Spe Salvi: On Christian Hope* (Washington, DC: United States Conference of Catholic Bishops—Libreria Editrice Vaticana, 2007), no. 3.

recognize that Christ came to give us the true freedom of the children of God. May we trust you in all the circumstances of life. Illumine the path before us and allow us to become the men and women you have always created us to be. We ask this in the name of Jesus Christ, our Lord. Amen.

CHAPTER 13

Proof for God

The Heartbeat of Hope

At 2:30 a.m., Mercy Hospital was normally steady and relatively quiet. The emergency room in New York City was likely to encounter almost anything, but rare were the nights that the experienced medical staff felt overwhelmed. Crisis management was simply a part of the skill set for the people who worked there. COVID-19 in the spring of 2020 changed that.

Sharon rushed from the ER to the ICU, breathless and exhausted like her patients. She was thinking about T.S. Eliot. More specifically, she was thinking about her freshman literature class at Providence College and the opening line to *The Waste Land*: "April is the cruellest month."[67]

---

67. T. S. Eliot, "The Waste Land," in *The Complete Poems and Plays* (New York: Harcourt Brace and Company, 1952), 37.

Eliot had been writing about World War I in Europe. With the melting snow, the pleasant weather ushered in a fresh season of military campaigns and a renewed slaughter that would claim countless lives. A century later, in this urban hospital in North America, another war was taking place. This virus that had quickly become a pandemic had already taken the lives of tens of thousands of people, with over 15,000 dying in New York City alone. There seemed to be no end in sight. The recent warmer weather was accompanied by tiny buds on the trees lining Mercy Hospital, but everywhere around her there were signs of death and not of life. *April is the cruellest month . . .*

Her faith had been strong when she was a young girl growing up in Westchester County. She had vivid memories of Sunday Mass with her mom and dad, her two little brothers teasing each other and often turning their playful childhood wrath on her. Sharon would sing extra loud, just to get even. She kept a prayer diary because that is what the saints did, and she desperately wished that she could someday become one. How excited she had been when, at twelve, she was chosen to crown the Blessed Virgin Mary on May Day! Somewhere in high school, though, things began to change. She never made a deliberate decision to stop praying or cease practicing her faith. There was no event that caused her to doubt her belief in God. Somehow, along the way, it just did not matter anymore.

Now, after two of the most overwhelming and difficult months in her nursing career, she hardly recognized that little girl from Westchester County. She had witnessed so much suffering, seen so many broken people, and felt so completely helpless to make any difference at all. She felt angry and guilty; guilty because she was angry, feeling sorry for herself when there were so many people with so much more to be sorry for.

About an hour before dawn, Sharon found an unused room down the hall from the ER. It had formerly been an ancillary waiting room, designed to take up the overflow of families and loved ones accompanying the sick and the dying. Now it was just a storage space for boxes of masks and gloves. She leaned her back against the wall and closed her eyes, tears blurring her vision behind her protective glasses. Sliding down into a sitting position, she let her tired head fall into her hands and sobbed uncontrollably. The same thought kept coming back to her, no matter how hard she tried to ignore it: *Why would God allow this to happen?* And then, another thought, or question, or suggestion, really. It was something that kept gnawing at her and left her anxious and afraid. She did not want to think about it, but the notion simply would not go away. *What if there actually is no God and we are all alone?*

✠ ✠ ✠

There are many different reasons people stop practicing their faith. Sometimes it is simply a matter of the busyness of daily life or misplaced priorities. For others, it could be that they lacked a firm foundation to begin with and were easily swept away by the fashions and fads of our fast-paced culture. For many, however, it is due to the often inexplicable nature of human suffering. When doubt is compounded with pain, it can be hard to know what to believe.

In the Prima Pars of the Summa Theologica, Saint Thomas Aquinas offers his famous five proofs for the existence of God. They are not proofs that describe what God is *like*, but simply reasonable arguments for accepting that God is real based upon what we can see and observe. For example, there is the *argument from motion*. Since we can observe that things have been set in motion, then there must be a Prime Mover, one who is not caused or moved by anything else. Then there is the *argument from design*. Animals, nature, and the world around us all seem to work according to a specific and observable purpose. Aquinas uses the analogy of an arrow hitting its target. It does not consider how this end will occur, but it reaches its mark because someone else directed it specifically to that place. The One who directs all things to their proper end, therefore, is God.

It is not common that hardened atheists will read the five proofs of Aquinas and immediately kneel to offer a heartfelt prayer of faith. Nonetheless, the five proofs provide a very sound and logical foundation, from the perspective of reason and common sense, for believing that God exists.

The problem of evil and suffering, however, provide an even more convincing foundation for believing that he does not! The experience of evil or suffering is not merely an intellectual exercise. No, it is a deeply personal encounter that resonates in the heart, mind, body, and soul of the person. When suffering is experienced on a deep and devastating level, or perhaps less intensely but over a pervasive period of time, one's faith in God can unravel as the suffering person becomes isolated from everything that once seemed so certain and secure.

As we have seen earlier, the philosophical and theological definition of evil is *privation*; it is a lack of a proper good where a good ought to be. There is no more common or convincing argument used down through the ages to deny the existence of God than the experience of evil. The atheist is seldom the one who has sat down and read the Scriptures and the Summa Theologica; it is not often the one who has studied theology extensively and then come to the sad conclusion that the idea of God is simply untenable. It is the man or woman who has experienced hell here on earth who will sometimes say, "I cannot believe that God exists." It is often the person who has encountered a tragic or sudden loss or the one whose life seems to be falling apart without any rhyme or reason; that is the one who will say, "I refuse to believe in a God who has allowed this to happen."

Even as people of faith, we are often at a loss for words when confronted with an argument like that. But Saint Thomas Aquinas, in his *Summa contra Gentiles*, uses that same line of reasoning to argue *for* the existence of God! The saints are sometimes surprising, and Saint Thomas frequently so. He argues, rather shockingly: *Quia malum est, Deus est. If there is evil, there is a God.*[68]

If evil is a privation or lack of the good, then it can only exist if there is good. For example, sickness and disease are rightly experienced as a lack of health and soundness of body; pollution is recognized as a violation of the beauty of the created world. Disease and pollution, then, are privations of the good that *ought* to be there. Traditionally we understand God as the creator of all things, and Scripture tells us that when he made them they were good (see Genesis 1:4–31). If God made all that is good, then he must have within himself the fullness

68. *The Summa Contra Gentiles of St. Thomas Aquinas*, trans. the English Dominican Fathers (London: Burnes, Oates and Washbourne, 1928), 177.

of goodness. There would be no classification of good things if not for the supreme good who is God.[69] Because God is good and creation reflects his goodness, the world would be irrational if the senseless tragedies that arise were not resolved in the end. Human existence would be irrational if there were no difference between a life lived morally well and a life given over to evil. Intuitively we know that there is a strong difference between good and evil, yet we often see things in this world go unresolved. But if God exists and ordered the universe, we can logically recognize that there must be a reward for good and a final punishment for evil. There must be a healing of the distortions caused by the Fall. We can know that God will respond to the violence and suffering that occurs in the world we live in. He will set things straight and bring about justice after all the injustice that has taken place from the beginning of time. *If there is evil, there is a God.*

As people of faith, we believe that even now God is beginning to do just that. He is—even now—beginning to restore order, unity, and beauty to the world that we live in. We see that clearly in all four accounts of the Gospel. Jesus Christ frequently encounters evil—that privation of the good. He meets it head on . . . and heals it. Yet, so often, he does so in a rather peculiar way.

Christ not only speaks the words of healing to broken people in the Gospels. Time after time, he also touches them. We are body and soul, and thus Christ heals those who are suffering both physically and spiritually at the point of their greatest need. The *Catechism of the Catholic Church* says that Christ, who consistently reaches out and touches those who

---

69. *Summa Contra Gentiles*, 177.

are broken and hurting in the Gospels, continues to touch us in the sacraments in order to heal us.[70] Thanks be to God for the Church that Christ founded!

Of course, this is not to say that the Church herself is without blemish in respect to her members. We know all too well, from the clerical abuse scandals to the common struggles with sin that are so evident every day, that the members of the Church are far from perfect. The Second Vatican Council teaches clearly that "the Church, embracing in its bosom sinners, at the same time holy and always in need of being purified, always follows the way of penance and renewal."[71] That need for penance and purification is especially pronounced when we reflect upon the times that members of the Church have chosen evil and caused suffering for many. Sometimes the very leaders of the Church who are called to help alleviate the suffering of God's people become the source of pain and division by their cooperation with evil, and the darkness of scandal falls upon the body of Christ. The mercy of God, however, does not cease to function even in our dysfunction. It is precisely because of the grace of God and the power of the Holy Spirit that the sacraments of the Church remain valid, even when the Church's members are imperfect. God never leaves us without a source of healing, and he never gives up on his plan to bring that healing to the world through the Church.

---

70. *Catechism of the Catholic Church*, no. 1504.

71. The Second Vatican Council, *Lumen Gentium*, The Holy See, November 21, 1964, https://www.vatican.va/archive/hist_councils/ii_vatican_council/documents/vat-ii_const_19641121_lumen-gentium_en.html, no. 8.

Thanks be to God for the sacraments by which Christ continues to reach out and touch this world so affected by evil and so much in need of healing and wholeness! The sacraments, of course, are not magic, nor are they the total solution to the problem of evil. They are a particular presence of Christ in the world, however, coming to us through the medium of human cooperation and love. Men and women open themselves to receiving these gifts from God, and the sacraments come to us through the hands of the priests or the ministers of the Church who have generously placed themselves at the service of the salvation Christ came to grant us. We could nuance the great argument of Saint Thomas Aquinas just a bit and say, *"Quia malum est, ecclesia est!"* If there is evil, there is a Church!

✠ ✠ ✠

Sharon remained on the floor of the ER storage room for several minutes, listening to the constant bustle around her. Glancing up, she saw another elderly person being brought in on a stretcher. Following behind the small entourage of medical personnel she saw something else that had been present throughout this ordeal, but something she had mentally dismissed. It was the hospital chaplain, completely equipped with protective gear and constantly carrying with him a prayer booklet and a few other items that were part of his kit. Instinctively, Sharon gathered her emotions, raised herself, and made her way to the corridor.

Standing outside the glass in the ICU, she could see her colleagues working furiously to keep this struggling patient alive. She did not need to be in there to know exactly what was happening. Like so many other healthcare workers, she had put her life on the line in these nightmarish months to help those who were so helpless. But why was the priest in there? That was a question she had considered many times during this crisis, but it was never the most important concern. Now it was.

She watched him with that interest children have when seeking to understand the strange and foreign habits of their parents. She knew the chances of survival for this patient. Why was the chaplain there at all? Something about the purple cloth draped over his neck, barely visible through the plastic, reignited some distant memory. He was now awkwardly making the sign of the cross on the patient's forehead with a blue plastic glove. All at once, Sharon realized what was happening, remembering what the priest was there for. And with that, began to remember who she was.

Several more colleagues had crowded in beside her without her realizing it. Their physical presence was a comfort, a gift. A moment of peace fell upon her, and warm tears welled up in her eyes. The monitor began to flatline moments after the priest had finished his ceremonious intervention, but Sharon felt a strange sense of trust that something significant had just taken place. She moved her hand toward her face to wipe away the tears but instead touched her forehead with two fingers, and then moved them down to her heart. Finishing that familiar, if forgotten, movement across her shoulders, she began to weep for sorrow and for joy.

1. Has the evil I have witnessed ever made me doubt the existence of God or call into question the goodness of creation?

2. Where have I experienced Christ's presence and healing touch in the sacraments or elsewhere in my life?

3. Has the Church been a source of healing and strength-
   for me in my suffering, or do I struggle to make this
   connection?

*O GOD, ALMIGHTY FATHER, you are the Author of our faith
and our salvation. When we encounter evil we often falter and
are beset by doubts. Help us to know that you have created us for
good and that you have a plan for our lives. May we recognize
your presence in the people we encounter and especially in the
sacraments of the Church, so that we can begin to experience the
healing touch of the redemption. We ask this in the name of Jesus
Christ, our Lord. Amen.*

CHAPTER 14

The Broken Road

A Way for the Church

The year was 386 and Augustine was grateful for the use of a friend's estate in the countryside near Milan. Several friends accompanied him, but none could provide relief from the heavy burden that he carried. "The Enemy kept his hold on my powers of willing," he would later write, "and had made of it a chain for me, and bound me with it."[72] It was an unholy bond that Augustine himself had helped forge. Beginning when he was a young man, in a year spent in idleness and lust while awaiting studies in Carthage, he had allowed bad habits to form and vice to flourish. When he finally entered that city he continued his sinful pursuits. Augustine began a relationship with a concubine, and she bore him a son, whom they

---

72. Saint Augustine, *The Confessions*, trans. and ed. Philip Burton (New York: Knopf, 2001), 168.

named Adeodatus, or "gift of God." Nonetheless, he remained far from that God whose intimacy he would later write about with tremendous passion.

One year after the birth of his son, Augustine became deeply immersed in philosophy. He spent hours reading Cicero, eventually showing himself proficient not only as a student but above all as a teacher. Becoming expert in rhetoric, an essential skill for the politics of the Empire, he was appointed imperial professor of rhetoric in Milan.

There was another desire that soon accompanied Augustine, however, and it grew deeper each day. It was the desire for God. No matter how strongly he felt that desire, he knew he would be unable to embrace it fully in his present state. It was not a lack in God's love that held him back, but a weakness within himself that kept him bound. In his own words, he was a slave to lust, and until free he could not commit himself to baptism and the full renunciation of sin.[73]

Now at the villa he was a man trapped between two worlds, desperately longing to be free. As he and his friend Alypius passed the time in discussion, a mutual acquaintance entered the room. Inquisitively, his eyes fell upon a book beside Augustine. He reached for the volume, supposing it to be a text on rhetoric or philosophy, but was surprised to find that Augustine had been poring over the Letters of Saint Paul. The acquaintance then told them the story of two close officials of the Emperor who had heard of the conversion of Saint Anthony and suddenly gave up everything to follow Christ.

Augustine became distraught. He rushed out into the garden, as Alypius followed close behind. Augustine could not bare his soul to his friend and felt it necessary to move

---

73. Saint Augustine, *The Confessions*, 130.

some distance away. It was then that he began to weep and lament alone. So had his own mother, Monica, wept for the conversion of her son. She had feared that the sordid life that had gripped him so tightly would finally become his ruin. She had turned to Ambrose, the Bishop of Milan, and pleaded with him to speak to her son; Augustine, in fact, had listened attentively to Ambrose's sermons many times. What would it cost to simply speak with this troubled young man? The saintly prelate had replied in the negative, insisting, "It is impossible that the son of these tears should perish."[74]

Yet here he was, on the verge of perishing, while at the same time on the edge of giving himself entirely to God. "Such was the sickness and torment that I knew," he relates, "twisting and turning in my bonds until such a time as they should be broken utterly; for now they held me only by a thread."[75]

Throwing himself now fully into the tears that had flooded his soul, Augustine pleaded with heaven and raged against the chain that bound him. He had not the strength to break it, but God did. Suddenly he heard a child's voice nearby, chanting, "Take up and read . . . take up and read." He took it to be the summons of God and thus returned to the volume with the Letters of Saint Paul; it was lying next to Alypius. He opened it at random and his eyes fell upon the words: "Let us conduct ourselves becomingly as in the day, not in reveling and drunkenness, not in debauchery and licentiousness, not in quarreling and jealousy. But put on the Lord Jesus Christ, and make no provision for the flesh, to gratify its desires" (Romans 13:13–14).

---

74. Saint Augustine, *The Confessions*, 61.

75. Saint Augustine, *The Confessions*, 180.

The spell was lifted. A terrible, manly vice was broken by a child's voice and the strength of the word of God. From that moment, he was certain that the chains of his unchastity were to be thrown off. He shared immediately with Alypius that he intended to be baptized. His friend, who had borne his own struggles, would also follow him to the font. They both went to share the news with Monica, whose tears of sorrow were turned to tears of joy.

Once back in the city, they enrolled in instruction for baptism and began their formal journey. Augustine was again acquainted with the inspiring sermons of Ambrose. It was Easter 387 when he received Baptism, along with his son and Alypius. It had not been a decision made in isolation. Augustine's entrance into the Christian faith had been cultivated by the wisdom of philosophy and theology, watered by the tears of Saint Monica, and seasoned with the sage sermons of Saint Ambrose. It was supported by the friendship of Alypius and embraced by the entire Christian community of Milan in the spring of 387.

✠ ✠ ✠

In *Salvifici Doloris*, John Paul II articulates the urgency with which the Church must embrace the suffering person as an expression of her evangelistic mission. Reflecting on his first encyclical, *Redemptor Hominis*, he says, "In Christ, 'every man becomes the way for the Church.'"[76] This expression—man, a way for the Church—sets the background for understanding how the individual suffering person can find

---

76. Saint John Paul II, *Salvifici Doloris*, no. 3.

consolation and transformation in Christ through his body, the Church.

Essentially, humanity is the route that the incarnate Christ traveled in fulfilling his salvific mission here on earth. He was born a child in the cave at Bethlehem and grew up in a community of love. Jesus worked with his hands and "dwelt among us" (John 1:14). He healed the sick and strengthened the weary with his words until he finally took our humanity to the cross on Calvary. Christ lived to the fullest the human life that he chose to share with us. Therefore, the Church can choose no other way in fulfilling the same mission entrusted to her.

When the Messiah walks into this world, he starts on the dark and broken road, and brings light to the suffering person. He has called the Church to that same mission. Augustine was a "slave to lust,"[77] but how many people find themselves enslaved by loneliness, mistakes of the past, or crippling fears about the future? How many find themselves beaten down by physical or mental illness? How many men and women walk the broken road in our own day? The Church serves to meet the broken person where he or she is and walks with them all in their suffering.

"The Church," says Saint John Paul II in *Redemptor Hominis*, "wishes to serve this single end: that each person may be able to find Christ, in order that Christ may walk with each person the path of life."[78] Christ, who reveals the truth about God and the truth about man, manifests himself to us

---

77. Saint Augustine, *The Confessions*, 130.

78. Saint John Paul II., *Redemptor Hominis*, The Holy See, March 4, 1979, no. 13, https://www.vatican.va/content/john-paul-ii/en/encyclicals/documents/hf_jp-ii_enc_04031979_redemptor-hominis.html.

as man when he takes on our humanity and then redeems that humanity through suffering on the cross. This infinite gift of the love of God in Christ encompasses all humanity and is extended to all persons for all times; it finds a fitting and particular place, it seems, in the life of the suffering person.

There is a paradox that is common to us all. We feel called to greatness and to a boundless existence, yet we also experience the pain of the world of suffering: our limitations, internal divisions, and societal discord. Saint John Paul II says that it is this very paradox that entails the way for the Church:

> This man is the way for the Church—a way that, in a sense, is the basis of all the other ways that the Church must walk—because man—every man without any exception whatever—has been redeemed by Christ, and because with man—with each man without any exception whatever—Christ is in a way united, even when man is unaware of it: 'Christ, who died and was raised up for all, provides man'—each man and every man—'with the light and the strength to measure up to his supreme calling.'[79]

The role of the Church, then, is to assist the suffering person in turning his or her gaze toward Christ, the Redeemer, and that heavenly calling Christ has come to reveal to the world. One of the primary ways this happens is through the proclamation of the Gospel, the "explicit proclamation of Jesus as Lord" and "the joyful, patient and progressive preaching of the saving death and resurrection of Jesus Christ."[80] Members of the Church need to be immersed in

---

79. Saint John Paul II., *Redemptor Hominis*, no. 14.

80. Pope Francis, *Evangelii Gaudium: The Joy of the Gospel* (Washington, D.C.: United States Conference of Catholic Bishops— Libreria Editrice Vaticana, 2013), no. 110.

this saving message and be ready to share it freely and lovingly with those around us. In a more formal and no less spontaneous way, this proclamation also must happen every Sunday when the Church is gathered to worship the living God. The word of God is broken open and Sacred Scriptures come alive as God deeply desires to speak to his people. When souls that are suffering truly hear the authentic message of the Gospel, they come to experience healing and new life. A good Christ-centered homily can make a world of difference to someone who is struggling to find meaning and hope, as it did in the life of Saint Anthony or Saint Augustine.

Another source of healing and renewal for suffering persons, and a place that becomes a way for the Church, is the Sacrament of Reconciliation. Saint Josemaría Escrivá would often say, "Play the role of the prodigal son every day."[81] That drama of being reconciled with our loving Father is one that can and should take place daily in prayer, but it is celebrated in a particular way in this sacrament that Christ instituted for the healing of sins. Perhaps nowhere else is the paradox of human life experienced more than in this sacrament. We come to Christ wounded and broken, and we receive the grace of forgiveness and renewal that places us back on the path of sanctification.

The place *par excellence* that the suffering person becomes a way for the Church is through the ordinary, everyday encounters with the members of the body of Christ. This might happen through grief support groups or other formal ministries, but it should also take place at work and in social

---

81. Saint Josemaría Escrivá, *Friends of God* (Princeton, N.J.: Scepter, 1981), 340.

settings, wherever Christians are immersed in the world in which we live. *Salvifici Doloris* dedicates its closing section to the Parable of the Good Samaritan, that thoughtful soul who stopped by the side of the road and helped a man who was robbed, beaten, and left for dead. Too many people today suffer without the support and solidarity they need to make it on the road to healing. The Church stands in a unique position to succor the suffering with the salve of charity.

Thus the Church's mission to the suffering person is to assist in that dialogue of love that clears the way for union with the person of Christ the Redeemer. All of this takes place through the assistance and the grace of the Holy Spirit. The Spirit, at work in the depths of the suffering person, is the same Spirit who made known the depths of divine love in the crucified and risen Christ. Gathering with his disciples on the night before he died, Jesus promised the Holy Spirit would be with them and comfort them through the difficult days ahead. The Holy Spirit dwells within the Christian community, animating and inspiring all of our works and words. He can act as a divine Liaison, connecting the Church with suffering souls and assuring those who struggle that they are not alone.

Where is Alypius, or Saint Monica, or Saint Ambrose today? Something as simple as lifting up a book and sharing a conversation with someone who is struggling could change his or her life forever. Today, more than ever, the Church needs to find the broken road and walk in it with the suffering person.

1. Have I ever had an encounter with the Church "on the broken road" of suffering?

2. How is God inviting me to walk with and bring consolation to others who are suffering?

3. Where does the Church need to be more attentive to the suffering person today? What are some concrete steps we can take that could make that a reality?

O GOD, ALMIGHTY FATHER, you see us from afar and draw near to us in the person of Christ and in the Holy Spirit. Illumine our hearts and help us to see that you are present to us in the members of your Church and in the sacraments that Christ instituted for our healing. Strengthen us and send us forth as wounded healers in a broken world that is constantly searching for you. We ask this in the name of Jesus Christ, our Lord. Amen.

CHAPTER 15

Now I Begin

Finding the Courage to Persevere

Few feel the fall from grace more painfully than those who have once soared as high as the heavens. In her early twenties, Saint Teresa of Avila had had powerful tastes of contemplation and the life of union with God. While she had experienced the cross significantly in those younger years, she had also received consoling spiritual gifts. Through no great fault or grave sin, she had slowly let them all slip away. Not being attentive to venial sins, she later recalled, nearly became her undoing.[82]

One of the strongest attachments, even for the saints during their earthly lives, is human affection. We all like to be

---

82. *The Collected Works of St. Teresa of Avila*, trans. Kieran Kavanaugh, O.C.D., and Otilio Rodriguez, O.C.D., vol. 1, *The Book of Her Life* (Washington, DC: ICS Publications, 1987), 67.

loved, appreciated, honored. When that affection and attach-
ment takes on a life of its own, however, it should come as no
surprise that God is no longer at the center of our lives. Saint
Teresa struggled to maintain a close relationship with the
Lord as a result of the distractions she allowed to capture her
attention. For most contemplatives, there is a cloister or
enclosure that separates them from the outside world and
allows them to focus more completely on God. In sixteenth-
century Spain, the cloister where Teresa began her religious
life was much more porous; visitors could come and go almost
as they pleased. Reforming this problematic aspect of the
Carmelite cloister would later be her signature work. For now,
however, the potent combination of the sheer number of
guests that the monastery received and Teresa's irresistible
personality added up to one of the greatest struggles of her
life. She was receiving frequent adulation from the people
around her but had grown far from God. That distance would
become a burden too heavy for her contemplative heart to
bear. What consolation is having many acquaintances when
you feel like you are losing the best friend you ever had?

From the time she was young, Teresa had always had a
deep devotion to the greatest of sinners who had become
saints. "The Magdalene" and Saint Augustine were at the top
of her list. "But there was one thing that left me inconsolable,"
she writes, "and that was that the Lord had called them only
once, and they did not turn back and fall again; whereas in my
case I had turned back so often that I was worn out from it."[83]
It was a battle she was to fight for over eighteen years.

However irresistible Teresa may have been to those
around her, there was within her an even greater interior

---

83. Saint Teresa of Avila, *The Book of Her Life*, 103.

attraction that drew her, which she was helpless to resist. God persistently pursued her for close to two decades and passionately sought this dove that had fallen from the heights countless times. For her, however, the weariness continued. In those vulnerable moments when she opened her heart to God in prayer, she often found the experience to be painful and even one that required courage. She had been chosen and called to be detached from the world and to live the intimacy of contemplation, but when she failed to honor that intimacy because of worldly attachments, she felt she was turning her back on God. "Though I continued to associate with the world," she explains, "I had the courage to practice prayer. I say courage, for I do not know what would require greater courage among all the things there are in the world than to betray the king and know that he knows it and yet never leave His presence."[84] Of course, we are always in the presence of God. Teresa above all persons realized that. Yet, she insists, it is different for those who practice prayer, for they are aware that God is looking at them.

At first, this conclusion on prayer sounds quite negative and even spiritually unhealthy. For Teresa, though, it became the defining experience of her relationship and friendship with God. Falling under that gaze of almighty God, she began to find courage and freedom. As she continued to return to prayer, again and again she found love in the gaze she received from God.

While her autobiography was written out of obedience and was read widely by an audience she would never meet, *The Way of Perfection* came by way of request from the sisters with whom she lived. In that deeply personal work, she describes

---

84. Saint Teresa of Avila, *The Book of Her Life*, 95.

the heart of prayer for this community she loved so dearly. She writes, "I am not asking you now that you think about Him or that you draw out a lot of concepts or make long and subtle reflections with your intellect. I am not asking you to do anything more than look at Him. For who can keep you from turning the eyes of your soul toward this Lord, even if you do so just for a moment if you can't do more? You can look at very ugly things; won't you be able to look at the most beautiful thing imaginable? Well now, daughters, your Spouse never takes His eyes off you."[85]

Not only had she been consoled in that tremendous gaze of love, but she longed for nothing else than to share that experience with her sisters. She encourages them—and us—to look right back at this God who transforms us by his gentle, forgiving, and loving gaze.

✠ ✠ ✠

We all long for a more intimate encounter with God, but often our sins can discourage us from seeking his face. The passion of the saints is to know and love God, and their ardor is contagious. They teach us that God is often working deeply in our lives and waiting patiently for us to recognize his gentle and loving gaze. But we often remain cold and distant from the God who is more intent upon intimacy than we can possibly imagine. Practically speaking, how can the spark of love catch flame in our everyday lives?

85. *The Collected Works of St. Teresa of Avila*, trans. Kieran Kavanaugh, O.C.D. and Otilio Rodriguez, O.C.D., vol. 2, *The Way of Perfection* (Washington, DC: ICS Publications, 1980), 133–134.

The Church professes and acknowledges the Holy Spirit to be "the Lord, the giver of life." Saint John Paul II describes the Church's essential role as witness and co-worker with the Holy Spirit in giving life to the world. Souls are given new spiritual life when the Church cooperates with the powerful work of the Holy Spirit. He says that it is precisely through this service to the suffering soul that the Church becomes "supremely aware" of the inner reality of the human person, "what is deepest and most essential in man, *because it is spiritual and incorruptible.*"[86]

The new life we receive from God, revealed in the salvific suffering, death, and resurrection of Jesus Christ, is not merely corporeal but also spiritual. This gift of new life necessarily relies on the grace and power of the Holy Spirit to reach the depths of the human person, and, in particular, the depths of the suffering person. John Paul II highlights this significant aspect of redemptive suffering, noting how Christ is able to lead and guide the suffering person through the heart of his own suffering. "Suffering cannot be *transformed* and changed by the grace from outside, but *from within*. And Christ through His own salvific suffering is very much present in every human suffering, and can act from within that suffering by the powers of His Spirit of truth, His consoling Spirit."[87] Redemptive suffering, therefore, relies on the gaze of God and the compassion of the Holy Spirit. Through this experience and inner transformation, says Saint John Paul II, the

---

86. Saint John Paul II, *Dominum et Vivificantem: The Holy Spirit in the Life of the Church and the World* (Boston: Pauline Books and Media, 1986), no. 58.

87. Saint John Paul II, *Salvifici Doloris*, no. 26.

human person begins to live in God, and God lives in that person; one begins to understand oneself and humanity in a whole new way.

The indwelling of the Holy Spirit makes us more aware of ourselves and how very much we are loved by God. We are also more sensitive to the suffering of those around us and more docile to the way the Spirit is moving us to go beyond ourselves. We become wounded healers, beggars ready to tell other beggars where we have found bread. Following the model, guidance, and interior presence of Christ, the suffering person is able to make that same self-gift that Christ made. In that offering of oneself to God and others, he or she discovers more completely the great dignity belonging to the children of God and even the hope of future glory.[88] The Second Vatican Council document *Gaudium et Spes* succinctly states one of the foundational dimensions of the human person: that "man, who is the only creature on earth which God willed for itself, cannot fully find himself except through a sincere gift of himself."[89] This self-gift is an essential dimension of redemptive suffering, although it depends upon perseverance and the courage to remain in the presence of God despite our vulnerabilities and failings.

In the early nineteenth century, the founder of the Oblates of the Virgin Mary, Venerable Bruno Lanteri, was captivated by a verse in the Vulgate version of the Bible. It was Psalm 77:10, and the translation at the time read *nunc coepi*, or "now

---

88. Saint John Paul II, *Dominum et Vivificantem*, no. 59.

89. Second Vatican Council, *Gaudium et Spes*, The Holy See, December 7, 1965, no. 24, https://www.vatican.va/archive/hist_councils/ii_vatican_council/documents/vat-ii_const_19651207_gaudium-et-spes_en.html.

I begin." It signaled a transformation in the psalmist's understanding that would inspire a new outlook and a change of
heart. Lanteri used it as a call to renewal as he encouraged
those around him to continually return to the Lord despite
their personal weaknesses and failings. The motto *nunc coepi*
has been taken up by various figures in recent times, from
Saint Josemaría Escrivá to former NFL quarterback Philip
Rivers, as they seek to answer the Lord's call to perseverance
and hope.

Suffering is a long and arduous journey, and it often
reveals the flaws and weaknesses that were already present in
our lives when we began to follow Christ. Hidden in that
spiritual struggle for harmony and peace lies the powerful
grace of God and the necessity for us to get back up and begin
again. Christ founded the Church to provide every possible
encounter to renew the weary soul and reignite the spark of
hope that suffering so often seems to smother. The Holy Spirit
constantly seeks to fan into flame that fire of love and light of
faith that is always near to those who carry the burden of the
cross.

The path of discipleship in Christ facilitates the encounter
with God that must mark every Christian journey. In the Acts
of the Apostles, we read about how the nascent Church
"devoted themselves to the apostles' teaching and fellowship,
to the breaking of the bread and the prayers" (Acts 2:42). Do
we have confidence today that these same elements can bring
healing to a broken world? The teachings of our faith and the
Eucharist have always been a wellspring for souls and never
grow old. Perhaps one of the most pressing needs today, however, is for souls to imitate the early Church's insistence on
attending to the life of prayer. The *Catechism of the Catholic
Church* says that "we pray as we live, because we live as we

pray."[90] How desperately the Church needs to rediscover the joy and inspiration of prayer today as in every age! Our daily conversation with God can become the source of inner transformation that we long for. Certainly there are obstacles, as there were for all the saints. Coming to realize that God is within our souls, awakening us to love and inspiring us to begin again, we rediscover the heart of the Christian life. We become aware, once again, that we fall under the loving gaze of almighty God and that he is waiting for us to return that look of love. Prayer nurtures the soul and helps us to grow and flourish in our faith and daily challenges. It is prayer that allows the suffering soul to find courage and faith to weather the storms of life and to know that it is not alone.

"I recount this also," writes Saint Teresa, "that one may understand how if the soul perseveres in prayer, in the midst of the sins, temptations and failures of a thousand kinds that the devil places in its path, in the end, I hold as certain, the Lord will draw it forth to the harbor of salvation as—now it seems—He did for me. May it please His Majesty that I do not get lost again."[91]

1. Have I ever experienced a time when the Holy Spirit consoled me or comforted me in the midst of difficulties? What helped facilitate that?

2. What is my initial reaction when I struggle to pray? How might Jesus want me to approach prayer, especially during times when prayer is difficult?

90. *Catechism of the Catholic Church*, no. 2725.

91. Saint Teresa of Avila, *The Book of Her Life*, 95–96.

3. What are some of the most helpful ways that I have found to "begin again" after failure or disappointment? Is there anything I could do differently going forward?

O GOD, ALMIGHTY FATHER, the sorrows and disappointments of this life can often discourage us and cause our hearts to falter. We seek the shelter and the calm that only you can give. Grant us the strength and courage to begin again, knowing that you are always ready to receive us. Lead us to the safe harbor of salvation and help us to be your instruments in the lives of all who suffer. We ask this in the name of Jesus Christ, our Lord. Amen.

CHAPTER 16

Presence and Participation

God Working in and Through Our Suffering

In the fifth century, as the Christian faith continued to spread throughout the world, a young man named Patrick was living in Britain. When he was sixteen, the village where he resided was attacked by marauders. Patrick was carried off to Ireland and forced to work as a shepherd. There, tending the flocks alone day after day, he began to remember the Catholic faith that he had been taught as a child but never completely followed. He remembered the exhortations to always be prepared for the day of salvation, to follow the commandments, to pray and worship God.

There, in the land of his exile, the light of faith was rekindled in the heart of that young man. He began to devote many hours each day to prayer. And so it was that Patrick was attentive to the voice of God within his soul. He conversed with God often and with a depth that reached well beyond his years. One evening, he heard the Lord say to him, "Behold, thy ship is ready."[92] It seemed quite strange to Patrick, because he was hundreds of miles from the shore! Nonetheless, he heard the voice again, "Thy ship is ready." Motivated by faith, he escaped from his captivity and made his way to the sea. He arrived just as a ship was leaving the port for Britain! Patrick was carried back home and was eventually reunited with his family.

✠ ✠ ✠

In the terminology of the international organizations, "forced migration" is what happens when there is war or conflict and millions of people suffer. People who are not soldiers, not directly involved in the conflict, are "in the way" and are forced to make a choice. Either they move or they die. Often, with only the clothes on their back and whatever they can carry in their hands (which is often their smallest child), they leave their home and seek a safer place.

There are tens of millions of forced migrants in the world. Nearly half of them are "internally displaced persons" or IDPs. They have fled their home but remain in the same country. Their future is far from secure. About a quarter million persons are refugees, people who have fled their own country and

---

92. Sir Samuel Ferguson, *The Remains of St. Patrick, Apostle of Ireland, The Confessio and Epistle to Coroticus* (Dublin: Sealy, Bryers and Walker, 1888), 21.

are seeking refuge in a foreign land, where they have no citizenship, no resources, and very little hope. Millions of others are trafficked, collateral damage in the world of conflict and war.[93]

In the Sacred Scriptures, we listen to a tragic story of forced migration in the Book of the Prophet Isaiah. We hear about the "land of Zebulun and the land of Naphtali" (Isaiah 9:1). These two tribes of Israel were located in the far northwest region of the nation. Because they were on the border, they were much more vulnerable to attack than the interior tribes. In the eighth century before the birth of Christ, the major superpower of that part of the world was Assyria. Over the course of several years, they had invaded, destroyed, and conquered the land of Zebulun and the land of Naphtali. Thousands of people were carried away into exile and enslaved in Assyria, never to return home. Furthermore, the Assyrians sent thousands of their own people into Zebulun and Naphtali, to "colonize" that place and erase its former identity. The phrase used in Sacred Scripture, "Galilee of the nations," was not a positive one, but a term of scorn and derision (Isaiah 9:1).

By the time of Christ, the people of Israel were well aware of the tragic fate of Zebulun and Naphtali. It was a dark place on the face of the earth, a place many would have considered forsaken. But Isaiah reminds the people of God that they have *not* been forgotten! This land is not forsaken. The Messiah would walk into the middle of that place and shine the light of hope on all humanity. Isaiah prophesied:

---

93. See The UN Refugee Agency, "Global Report 2021," https://reporting.unhcr.org/globalreport2021/pdf.

In the former time he brought into contempt the land of
Zebulun and the land of Naphtali, but in the latter time he
will make glorious the way of the sea, the land beyond the
Jordan, Galilee of the nations.

> The people who walked in darkness
>   have seen a great light;
> those who dwelt in a land of deep darkness,
>   *on them light has shined. (Isaiah 9:1–2)*

Saint Matthew's Gospel proclaims that Jesus "went and
dwelt in Capernaum by the sea, in the territory of Zebulun
and Naphtali, that what was spoken by the prophet Isaiah
might be fulfilled" (Matthew 4:13–14). It is there in the "land
of deep darkness" that Jesus will call his first apostles, whom
he will send out to the farthest reaches of the world to spread
the light of the Gospel of salvation. God has indeed made
"glorious the way of the sea"!

The spiritual principle we find at work in the Sacred
Scriptures teaches us that God can—and often does—work
in the most painful places. He is capable of shining his light
into the darkness of our world in every age. The miracle of
grace that happened in the first century with the coming of
Christ continues to work in the world through his body, the
Church. This must be, in the words of Saint John Paul II, the
"way of the Church"[94] for those who find themselves in darkness and despair.

What becomes clear in Saint John Paul II's presentation
of the human person as "the way of the Church" is God's
desire to unite himself to every suffering person, especially
through the profound union between the believer and Christ.

---

94. Saint John Paul II, *Salvifici Doloris*, no. 3.

Because Christ has taken on himself the sins of all and redeemed all through suffering, every person has the capacity to share in that new life that springs from the risen Christ. The believer also shares, in the same way, in his redemptive suffering.[95]

This happens in two ways. Firstly, Christ has opened up his suffering to all by coming to share in our suffering condition. This suffering began long before Calvary. Very early in his life here on earth, while he was still a small child, Christ became a refugee on the flight to Egypt. Even as an adult, Christ "came to his own home, and his own people received him not" (John 1:11). Christ experiences human suffering on many levels and unites that suffering to love on the cross in obedience to the Father's will.

Secondly, we can now discover this redemptive suffering in our own lives, through faith. In faith we come to recognize the sufferings of Christ in our own personal experience.[96] The suffering person's encounter with the world of suffering is different now. One can now identify his or her very self with Christ in suffering, and find hope. The poor and the homeless are Christ, who has nowhere to lay his head. The grieving widow is Christ, who wept at the tomb of Lazarus. All unrequited love is Christ, rejected even in his hometown and ultimately turned over to be crucified in the passion. This recognition of Christ in our own experience, says Saint John Paul II, was Saint Paul's impetus for the bold proclamation he makes in his Letter to the Galatians: "I have been crucified with Christ; it is no longer I who live, but Christ who lives in

---

95. See Saint John Paul II, *Salvifici Doloris*, no. 19.
96. See Saint John Paul II, *Salvifici Doloris*, no. 20.

me; and the life I now live in the flesh I live by faith in the Son of God, who loved me and gave himself for me" (Galatians 2:20).

The New Testament expresses this concept in many places, and the focus is always on the resurrected Christ; it is the light of the resurrection shining on the darkness of suffering.[97] It is God on "the way of the sea."

One of the more profound passages where Saint Paul identifies himself and his readers with the sufferings of Christ is found in the fourth chapter of his Second Letter to the Corinthians. There Saint Paul talks about his apostolic ministry and the sufferings he experiences in the midst of it. He carries that ministerial treasure in the earthen vessel of his body, so prone to suffering and affliction. Identifying himself, as well as all who are engaged in the apostolic ministry, with the suffering Christ, Saint Paul says that they are "always carrying in the body the death of Jesus, so that the life of Jesus may be manifested in our bodies" (2 Corinthians 4:10). But in the middle of that reflection, Paul suddenly changes his focus, saying that death is certainly at work in them (those engaged in the apostolic ministry), but *life* is at work in the Corinthians. This shows us that our sufferings are not worthless nor useless when they are accepted in faith and united with Christ. They have the capacity to contribute mightily for the sake of others in ways that we could never fully imagine. We make an offering to God when we freely choose to unite our sufferings to Christ. Our Lord can take that offering and use it to bring about good, pouring out grace into the lives of those we love and even those we have never met.

---

97. See Saint John Paul II, *Salvifici Doloris*, 20.

In my life as a priest I have met many suffering people and have been encouraged by their devout desire to remain close to the suffering Christ, but perhaps the example that has affected me most profoundly was the endurance in love that I saw in my own mother. Afflicted with rheumatoid arthritis in her early thirties, she would become nearly crippled by that disease in a very short time. I have no memory of her not in physical pain. For over forty years, she suffered complications and setbacks, and yet she always maintained a vibrant and living faith in Jesus Christ. I do not think that my mother would have been able to articulate a theology of redemptive suffering if prompted, but she lived her life united to the cross of Christ and was an instrument for good in our world. Her constant sufferings were woven seamlessly into her daily devotion to the Eucharist, love for the Christian faith, and desire to do good for others. We will never know in this life how many graces and gifts my family or others in the world received from my mother's union with the cross of Christ, but we can be assured that none of our sufferings ever go to waste. God guards our suffering as a treasure and knows how to make the most out of all that we are willing to share with him.

None of us chooses to be poor, broken, discarded, or alone. Nobody desires to suffer in loneliness or to be rejected by others. We all long for health, well-being, and prosperity. But when we encounter the cross, we can be assured that God has already drawn close to us. What we cannot fully know is what God intends to accomplish with every act of love we offer to him in our suffering. Perhaps we will discover one day, in this life or in the next, the treasure that exists in the offering of love freely given.

✠ ✠ ✠

Several years after his return to Britain, Patrick heard another voice. This time it was not the voice of God, but the "voices of the Irish."[98] He heard these words deep within his soul: "Come, holy youth, and walk amongst us."[99] His heart was broken at the sound of these words, and he was moved with great love, choosing to return to Ireland as a missionary and to proclaim the Catholic faith to the Irish. It was fitting, because it was in Ireland that his relationship with God had truly taken root. His many years of suffering and toil, far from home, had opened up a space for God in his soul. He had been a shepherd in that foreign land, but now God was calling him back to be a shepherd of souls. Saint Patrick, as we know, is the patron saint of Ireland. In him, too, did God glorify "the way of the sea."

1. Is there any place in my life or in the world today that I can identify as a "land of gloom"? How might Christ shine a light into that darkness?

2. Have I ever been able to recognize Christ's sufferings in my or another person's sufferings?

3. What would it look like if I united my sufferings to the sufferings of the cross?

---

98. Ferguson, *The Remains of St. Patrick*, 24.

99. Ferguson, *The Remains of St. Patrick*, 24.

O GOD, ALMIGHTY FATHER, we sometimes feel like we are in the land of darkness and we long for your light and love. You sent your Son to dwell among us and to take on our suffering and sorrow. Teach us to recognize your Son in the sufferings we experience and help us to offer ourselves to you in love through all the contradictions in life. With you as our guide may we find true peace. We ask this in the name of Jesus Christ, our Lord. Amen.

CHAPTER 17

The Patience of God

Perseverance in the Face of Evil

One of the most compelling stories of forgiveness and grace is found in the person of Saint Maria Goretti. Maria was born in Ancona, Italy, in 1890. The Gorettis eventually moved to Nettuno, where they shared a house with Giovanni Serenelli and his son, Alessandro. The arrangement allowed both families to share the expenses while maintaining together the farm connected to their property.

Alessandro, although eight years older than Maria, developed a sinful desire for her and harassed her often with his unwanted sexual advances. Seeing her alone one day, he threatened her with violence if she did not give in to him. Maria outrightly refused, insisting, "It is a sin! God does not want this!"[100] There was never a question of sin on Maria's

---

100. Godfrey Poage, *St. Maria Goretti: In Garments All Red* (Charlotte, North Carolina: Tan Books, 1998), 37.

part: even if Alessandro had overpowered her, she would not have been complicit in his sin. Remarkably, she had the spiritual insight to recognize that Alessandro was cooperating with a sinful desire, and she wanted God's plan for his life. She courageously communicated this to him again and again. She also insisted that this sin would destroy him, and he would go to hell. In a rage, Alessandro turned on her and stabbed her multiple times, leaving her for dead.

Finding Maria bleeding to death on the floor of the house, the family brought her to the hospital, where the doctors operated on her without anesthesia. At one point, when asked about Alessandro, she replied, "For the love of Jesus I too pardon him, and I want him to be with me in heaven."[101] Maria died the next day. She was eleven years old.

✠ ✠ ✠

All of our lives are confronted, sooner or later, by the question of evil. Theology sometimes refers to it as the scandal of evil, because it is a reality that causes many to stumble in their faith and to become confused in their relationship with God. As we have seen, the *Catechism of the Catholic Church* insists that there is no quick answer or facile solution to this question. Instead, it provides a more comprehensive and even expansive explanation, one that includes the entire story of creation, the fall, redemption, and the final judgment:

> Only Christian faith as a whole constitutes the answer to
> this question: the goodness of creation, the drama of sin,

---

101. Godfrey Poage, *St. Maria Goretti*, 47.

and the patient love of God who comes to meet man by his covenants, the redemptive Incarnation of his Son, the gift of the Spirit, his gathering of the Church, the power of the sacraments, and his call to a blessed life to which free creatures are invited to consent in advance, but from which, by a terrible mystery, they can also turn away in advance.[102]

So much for quick solutions and easy answers! Basically, the entire Christian faith is alone sufficient to answer the question of evil. Importantly, the *Catechism* goes on to phrase that same answer in a manner that is even more compelling: "There is not a single aspect of the Christian message that is not in part an answer to the question of evil."[103]

An essential way of engaging that mystery, then, would be to avoid any immediate or hasty solutions and basically to live fully the Christian faith in the particular circumstances of one's life. That sounds rather simple, but in fact it is a very challenging thing to do. In particular, when we encounter the crosses of life or experience the question of evil in a particularly painful way, it requires faith and trust in God and dependency upon his amazing grace. Which brings us back to the story of Saint Maria Goretti.

Although Alessandro Serenelli was convicted and sentenced to thirty years in prison, he remained impenitent. Far from showing any signs of remorse, he was menacing to the guards who watched over him. One evening, about six years after he entered the prison, Alessandro had a dream where Maria appeared to him and offered him a bouquet of lilies. As he received those flowers, they immediately burst into flames

---

102. *Catechism of the Catholic Church*, no. 309.

103. *Catechism of the Catholic Church*, no. 309.

and turned to ashes in his hands. When he awoke, he took responsibility for what he had done and his life began to change completely.

After twenty-seven years, Alessandro was released from prison and he sought out Maria's mother, Assunta, to beg her for forgiveness. In the decades that had passed since the death of her beloved Maria, Assunta would have reflected often on the precious life that had been taken from her. How often she would have struggled with the bitterness and the loss! But she was also left with an example of love that shone through even in that grim hospital room in the final hours of Maria's life. Assunta considered how Maria, even as she lay dying, had forgiven Alessandro. She made the challenging decision to follow that same example. It was Christmas Eve, 1937. Not only did Assunta forgive him, but she also attended Midnight Mass with Alessandro, and the two knelt side-by-side at the communion rail to receive the Blessed Sacrament.

Pope Pius XII canonized Saint Maria Goretti in 1950, at that time one of the largest canonization celebrations in the history of the Church. Both Assunta *and* Alessandro were present.[104] Alessandro entered a Franciscan monastery after his imprisonment and spent his days caring for the garden there and seeking to devote himself to the Christian faith. He certainly would have been told Saint Maria's Goretti's dying words, how she had forgiven him for the love of Jesus and wanted him to join her in heaven. Alessandro spent the rest of his life seeking to make her desire a reality.

In Chapter 13 of Saint Matthew's Gospel, we are pre-sented with Jesus' challenging parable of the weeds and wheat.

---

104. Glynn MacNiven-Johnston, *Maria Goretti: Teenage Martyr* (London: Catholic Truth Society, 1997), 31.

The servants approach the owner of the field, recognizing that there are weeds among the wheat he had sown. The owner responds, "An enemy has done this" (Matthew 13:28). The servants are all too eager, of course, to solve that problem immediately. "Then do you want us to go and gather them?" they ask (Matthew 13:28). The householder responds, "No; lest in gathering the weeds you root up the wheat along with them" (Matthew 13:29). He insists, "Let both grow together until harvest" (Matthew 13:30).

The householder goes on to say that the *harvesters* will do the sifting at the harvest time, and they will separate the weeds from the wheat. Later, in the interpretation of that parable, Jesus indicates that the harvesters are the angels. Imagine, for a moment, if the harvesters never had the chance to sift through the life of Alessandro Serenelli. It would have been very easy, and perhaps would have even seemed just, if he had been condemned and forgotten in those years following the death of Saint Maria. But Maria herself was the first to have the compassionate spiritual insight that her attacker was a man worthy of grace and forgiveness. She saw the good that his soul was capable of receiving, and that he could be loved and saved by God. How much patience and forgiveness did Assunta require to remain steadfast in her own faith, and then to forgive the man who had taken away her daughter? How many others had looked upon Alessandro simply as a monster, and not a man worthy of life? Yet the drama of the Christian faith, in all its many facets, was being lived out in the circumstances that unfolded.

The drama of our own daily lives is no different. In his inaugural homily in April 2005, Pope Benedict XVI reflected on the mystery of evil and our need for patience when we encounter the trials of life. He spoke of how painful it can be to endure the misfortunes of evil, and how tempting it is for us to seek quick solutions. We long for God to show himself stronger, he explained, eliminating the problem of evil and immediately making the world a better place when, in actuality, this is the way that ideologies of power often act. An immediate judgment of the obstacles that stand in our way leads to rash decisions and often harmful consequences. We often experience suffering, Benedict indicates, as a result of God's patience in not directly intervening to stop evil from taking place, and yet we ourselves ultimately depend on the patience of God. What would our lives look like if we were to receive the immediate judgment of God in every circumstance? God is different than we are. He is patient, loving, and merciful, and we need that. "God, who became a lamb," Benedict concludes, "tells us that the world is saved by the Crucified One, not by those who crucified him. The world is redeemed by the patience of God. It is destroyed by the impatience of man."[105]

Living the Christian life does not exempt us from the problem of evil or the very real possibility of encountering human suffering. The Christian Faith as a whole, in fact, is what is necessary to respond to this demanding reality. We can be confident that God is with us in this struggle, helping us to overcome and to see the face of Christ even in the midst of life's trials and difficulties. The patience of God gives us courage to endure even the most bitter suffering, knowing

---

105. "Homily of His Holiness Benedict XVI," The Holy See, April 24, 2005, https://www.vatican.va/content/benedict-xvi/en/homilies/2005/documents/hf_ben-xvi_hom_20050424_inizio-pontificato.html

that Christ will transform our crosses into moments of grace and new life.

1. Have I ever suffered because of the patience of God, waiting for him to act in my life? What did I feel at the time? How do I feel about it now?

2. Can I point to examples in my life or in the world where bad situations turned out better over time?

3. When I reflect on the parable of the weeds and the wheat, what is my reaction to the owner's patience in not uprooting the weeds right away? How does the patience of God inspire me to approach the difficult situations in my life?

O GOD, ALMIGHTY FATHER, we are often overwhelmed by the evil that happens in the world and desire that you would act more quickly to bring us peace. Help us to wait upon your mercy and to see you acting in the concrete circumstances of our lives. May we have the gift of patient vigilance, watching for your Providence and living in your love. We ask this in the name of Jesus Christ, our Lord. Amen.

CHAPTER 18

Encounter
with the Living God

Sharing in the Suffering of Christ

One of the more dramatic scenes in the Acts of the Apostles is the conversion of Saint Paul. He has just obtained letters authorizing him to arrest Christians in Damascus and bring them bound to Jerusalem. Suddenly he is struck blind by a mysterious light and falls to the ground, hearing a voice saying to him, "Saul, Saul, why do you persecute me?" (Acts 9:4). Perplexed by the light and by the voice, Saul inquires who this person might be. The voice replies, "I am Jesus, whom you are persecuting" (Acts 9:5).

The Italian artist Caravaggio has two famous paintings of this scene. One simply shows Saul and the horse he has just fallen from. The other painting, however, is much busier! It reveals Saul, lying on the ground, his hands defensively shielding his eyes from the light. Christ appears above him, flanked by an angel. The Lord's hands are outstretched, beckoning to Saul. Some of Saul's companions, and even his horse, all look toward Christ in amazement. In that scene, Caravaggio has chosen to include beings that are divine, angelic, human, and animal. There is certainly a lot going on!

While the Acts of the Apostles makes no mention of a horse and the vision of Christ is not made visible to anyone but Saul, Caravaggio's interpretation rings true when it comes to the implications of Saul's persecution of the Church. The suffering he brings upon the followers of Christ has a ripple effect that reaches far and wide. Now he is confronted directly by God, who will respond to the question of suffering in one of the most personal and mysterious ways imaginable.

✠ ✠ ✠

The first time we see Saul witnessing pain and suffering in the Church is at the stoning of Saint Stephen. Saul not only approved of this act of violence but went on to afflict the Church in his own campaign against the followers of Christ. But it is on the road to Damascus, in the thick of this persecution, that Saul finally faces the suffering he has caused, and he faces it in a very personal way. He believes himself to be righteously pursuing the enemies of God as he attacks the Church, but he comes to discover that the members of this Way that he has been so zealously persecuting are identified with Jesus Christ himself. This encounter sets the stage for what will become Saint Paul's understanding of the Mystical Body of Christ, the Church.

In his Letter to the Ephesians, Saint Paul says that God has made Christ "the head over all things for the Church, which is his body, the fullness of him who fills all in all" (Ephesians 1: 22–23). What does it mean for Paul to say that the Church is the fullness (in Greek, *pleroma*) of Christ? This fullness does not signify an insufficiency in Christ, but is instead a way of describing his work in the members of the Church as they grow in sanctification. God will gradually fill the world with the love of Christ through the members of his body, the Church, allowing them to flower in divine grace through their cooperation with his plan for their lives. Saint Paul, when he speaks about the Church being the fullness of Christ, is proclaiming the victory of Christ over suffering and death and describing that victory now at work—though as yet incomplete—in the Church through the power of God.

This Church is what Saint Paul encounters even at the outset on the road to Damascus. The Risen Christ who reveals himself to Paul is yet still a suffering and persecuted Christ. He has certainly completed the work of the redemption at the cross, but that victory does not absolve his followers from continuing the battle. The Church is still engaged in a great struggle, which involves much suffering. Christ is calling Paul away from persecution and into the mystery of redemptive suffering, seeking to engage him actively in that struggle. This is the context in which Saint Paul speaks to the Colossians when he says, "I complete what is lacking in Christ's afflictions for the sake of his body, that is, the Church" (Col 1:24). It is not the case that there is something missing from the passion, or that the cross of Christ is somehow incomplete. Nothing more is awaited or necessary for us to be redeemed. Yet Christ has allowed room in his perfect work of redemption for us to participate and to encounter him at the very place where he has emptied himself out in love.

This is the context in which Saint John Paul II refers to the redemptive value of suffering as a good within the life of the Church. Of course, it bears repeating that suffering itself is always a negative experience and does not have value in and of itself. It is simply that Christ has redeemed suffering and opened up a way for us to share in his act of love on the cross. Saint John Paul II returns to the point made earlier, about how the world's Redemption was brought about through Christ's sufferings, which have now become a superabundant resource to all who suffer.[106] That love which annihilates evil and creates good[107] is not something Christ clings to but a good he shares freely with all who are able to embrace it. This is indicative of what Saint John Paul II calls the "creative character" of redemptive suffering. The redemption is not just a moment when Christ died on the cross; it continues by the grace of God and develops historically in every time and place.

While the creative character of redemptive suffering was certainly evident in the persecutions and sufferings of the early Church, it is no less active today in the members of the Mystical Body of Christ. Christ still leaves room for us to "complete what is lacking" by uniting our sufferings to his redemptive work on the cross. In no way does that diminish the painful significance of what we are going through. Quite the contrary: we come to see our own personal suffering in the rich light of the Christian faith. Christ, who draws near to all

---

106. Saint John Paul II, *Salvifici Doloris*, no. 24.
107. Saint John Paul II, *Salvifici Doloris*, no. 17.

who suffer, allows us to also unite ourselves to him more completely when we experience the cross.

The General Introduction for the *Pastoral Care of the Sick: Rites of Anointing and Viaticum* also expresses this creative character when it reminds those who suffer that sickness has a value and meaning not only for themselves but for the salvation of the world. It highlights that family members who are present to comfort and strengthen the sick should also encourage and assist them as they "contribute to the well-being of the people of God by associating themselves willingly with Christ's passion and death."[108]

This cooperation with the redemption through suffering is not easy or uncomplicated. Several years ago I was called to a hospice center to anoint a dying patient. When I arrived, the room was teeming with family members; there were more than a dozen people attentively supporting their loved one in those final moments. When I entered the room, most of them welcomed me with gratitude. One young man, however, immediately turned away and blankly stared out the window, his arms folded across his chest. While I was concerned for him and could not even begin to know what his feelings might be, I was there specifically to anoint his grandfather. No sooner did I finish giving the dying man the last rites when he stopped breathing and peacefully died. The family members noticed it immediately and wept tears of sorrow and relief that his physical suffering was now over. Out of the corner of my eye, I saw that young man who just moments

---

108. National Conference of Catholic Bishops, *Pastoral Care of the Sick: Rites of Anointing and Viaticum* (New York: Catholic Book Publishing Co., 1983), 30.

before had been looking out of the window. Now he was turned squarely toward his grandfather. With tears in his eyes he devoutly made the sign of the cross.

It is not only the physical suffering that we endure that allows us to "complete" the sufferings of Christ. There are many places in life where the cross is made manifest and we are given the chance to unite our brokenness and affliction to his. We are created for relationship, for example, but we often experience separation and conflict with those around us. Broken families, broken promises, and broken lives are common in the world in which we live. While we should always seek reconciliation when possible, in the end we might be left with no other recourse than to turn to the cross of Christ and unite ourselves lovingly to him. There are countless other ways the cross of Christ can enter our lives— financial loss, difficulty with employment, and so on—and in them all we are reminded that we can always make a choice. We can decide to unite ourselves to the suffering Christ, receiving the consolation that only he can give and discovering the surprising gift of participation in his redemption.

While it is true that the Church recognizes a special value in suffering as a good that participates in the very work of Christ's redemption,[109] this is not a perspective the suffering person acquires automatically. When Saint John Paul II first introduces the theme of redemptive suffering, citing Saint Paul's joy at this discovery in his own life, he quickly qualifies it by relating how this meaning of suffering is found "at the end of the long road."[110] This road, he indicates, winds its way

---

109. Saint John Paul II, *Salvifici Doloris*, no. 24.
110. Saint John Paul II, *Salvifici Doloris*, no. 1.

through human history and is illuminated by the word of God. It is sometimes only at the very end of the long journey with suffering that we begin to acquire the insights that allow us to be more intimately united to Christ and the power of the cross.

These words, especially true in the long journey of Saint Paul, reveal a certain "order" that necessarily involves an experience of the resurrection first. We must first experience the Risen Christ, says Saint John Paul II, and find the "salvific light" of his cross shining on the darkness of our own suffering before we can begin to see the redemptive meaning of human suffering.[111] In other words, we first encounter the joy of the Christian life and the power of forgiveness. We must first grasp how completely we are accepted and loved by God, how totally in love Christ is with each one of us. From there we begin to see that this love also involves the recognition that he is present to us not only in moments of tenderness and calm but also in the moments of darkness, emptiness, and pain. Christ shines his light into that darkness and allows us to see that he is with us and even inviting us to cooperate with him in the love that redeems the world.

Saint John Paul II does not offer any simplified solutions in the search for a personal meaning to one's suffering. Instead he points to a personal encounter with the risen Christ in which one discovers only gradually, over time, that God has come to us in our suffering and given us hope. Discovery of the meaning of redemptive suffering thus takes the form of a call, a vocation, and above all a response to the God who first calls us in his Son, Jesus Christ. Saint Paul recognized that

---

111. Saint John Paul II, *Salvifici Doloris*, no. 21.

call and it changed his life. As Caravaggio's painting reveals, however, the Apostle's experience of suffering and the redemption has broad implications. There is always a ripple effect, not just in suffering but especially in the redemption. The waves of suffering eventually touch every human life, but so does the tenderness of God.

1. Have I ever experienced a "Damascus moment" of encountering Christ in an unexpected way? How has this experience carried over into other areas of my life?

2. What are some of the insights I have learned on the "long road" or journey of my own sufferings?

3. Have I ever thought of sharing in Christ's redemptive suffering as a call or a vocation? Can I think of any concrete ways to live out this calling more intentionally?

O GOD, ALMIGHTY FATHER, we thank you that you have called us to participate in the life of Jesus, your Son. Thank you that he who is fully human and fully divine draws near to us in our suffering and gives us consolation and strength. Help us to hear his voice and respond generously to his call to intimacy and a sharing in the work of the redemption. We ask this in the name of Jesus Christ, our Lord. Amen.

CHAPTER 19

Suffering for Christ

The Cross of Martyrdom

The fires raged in Rome for days on end. Three districts were consumed entirely; another seven were severely damaged. The emperor was uneasy. It was not the spreading of the flames that bothered him but the accusations and the blame that were moving increasingly in his direction. Nero definitely needed a scapegoat. The anger and discontent of the masses would need to be assuaged. His clever mind deliberated, cunningly combing over every possibility. A sadistic smile spread across his face as his thoughts suddenly turned to that notorious sect called "Christians."

These followers of Jesus of Nazareth were already hated for their abhorrent behavior and peculiar principles. They held "love feasts" in which it was purported that they ate the flesh and drank the blood of their founder. Many considered them to be living incestuous lifestyles, for they referred to each other as brother and sister. Worse still, they were irreligious, since they did not practice the common worship of the Roman gods. Convincing the multitudes that these Christians were to blame would not be difficult at all.

Soon the conspiracy gained ground and spread like wildfire throughout the city. Nero wasted no time rounding up Christians for execution. Many were consigned to the arena. Covered in the skins of animals, they were savagely consumed by dogs and wild beasts. Others were systematically crucified, lining the roadways for all to see. Some were burned alive, displayed in the emperor's courtyard in the evening twilight as macabre lanterns while their anguished cries went unheeded.

It was then that Peter was arrested and brought to the Circus of Caligula. He was their leader and would provide a fitting testimony to Nero's twisted sense of justice. They were determined to crucify him, as would be a fitting execution for a follower of Christ. What surprise and wonder, though, when he refused the precise manner of torture to which he had been assigned. He insisted, instead, that he be crucified upside down, feeling himself unworthy to die in the same way as his Savior.

✠ ✠ ✠

In *Salvifici Doloris*, Saint John Paul II describes what he calls a "Gospel of Suffering"[112] that has been given to the Church through the death and resurrection of Christ. He says that Christ himself wrote this Gospel by his own suffering

---

112. Saint John Paul II, *Salvifici Doloris*, nos. 25–26.

accepted in love and that it has become a rich treasure for the disciples of Christ. Suffering, which is always associated with negativity, now forms part of the Good News of the resurrection and new life.

There are two "chapters" in the Gospel of Suffering, Saint John Paul II indicates, and the first one entails suffering specifically for the sake of Christ. Jesus foretells this particular form of suffering in the most direct way, leaving no room for doubt concerning its nature: "They will deliver you up to tribulation, and put you to death; and you will be hated by all nations for my name's sake" (Mt 24:9). He reminds his disciples, on the night before he suffers and dies, that "a servant is not greater than his master" (Jn 15:20) and that those who persecuted him would soon persecute them. "Indeed," he insists, "the hour is coming when whoever kills you will think he is offering service to God" (Jn 16:2). Persecution and martyrdom, therefore, are not merely collateral damage in the struggle to live an authentic Christian life. They are a full participation in the suffering and death of Jesus Christ. This Gospel of Suffering, writes Saint John Paul II, "contains in itself *a special call to courage and fortitude*, sustained by the eloquence of the resurrection."[113] It is not a suffering, then, without hope. If we share in the sufferings of Christ, we will also share in his resurrection (see Philippians 3:10).

The great testimony to courage and fortitude, buoyed by hope, has coursed down through the centuries as countless Christians have given their lives for the sake of the Gospel and as faithful witnesses to the Lord. In our own time it is no different. Hostility toward the Gospel message and the

---

113. Saint John Paul II, *Salvifici Doloris*, no. 25.

followers of Christ takes many forms in the world we live in. Standing up for what one believes in could result in unemployment or exclusion from mainstream social circles. Christian businesses are being forced to cater to the permissive and even decadent culture or risk dealing with legal ramifications. Simply holding on to the beautiful teachings of our faith on human sexuality and marriage often bring us into conflict with the people around us.

In other parts of the world, however, the stakes are significantly higher. One need only look at the Church that is suffering greatly in parts of Africa, the Middle East, and other areas of the world. The stories of the martyrs are not stories of years gone by; they are the stories that are being written today. Often they do not even make the evening news, the violence is so commonplace. Yet the Gospel of Suffering continues to be written.[114]

On February 15, 2015, a chilling event happened on the shores of Libya. A video released by ISIS showed twenty-one men wearing orange jumpsuits being marched out in single file along a beach. Each of them was accompanied by a masked ISIS militant. They were Egyptian migrant workers kidnapped several months before. The leader of the militants declared that they were to be executed because they were "people of the cross." Twenty of them were Coptic Christians from Egypt. The last one was a migrant worker from Ghana; he was given a chance to escape the grim fate that awaited them. It is reported that he responded, "I am a Christian and I am like them." They all died together, beheaded for their belief in Jesus Christ.

114. Saint John Paul II, *Salvifici Doloris*, no. 26.

A tragedy that happened in Yemen in March 2016, however, has the potential to open our hearts to the surprising truth about God in the midst of the mystery of human suffering and in the face of evil. But first, it is helpful to understand some of the more recent history of Yemen. The country is located in the southern region of the Middle East and has been beset by civil strife and unrest since 2011. Caritas Internationalis, other international aid organizations, and many different religious groups have done tremendous work to help the people of Yemen, but the needs there are still great. One of those groups is the Missionaries of Charity, the order founded by Saint Teresa of Calcutta. They operated a hospital in Yemen for elderly and disabled persons. They were warned many times that their ministry was in a dangerous and volatile place, but they refused to leave the sick and suffering persons under their care. Father Tom, an Indian priest who celebrated daily Mass for them, would often say that they should be prepared for martyrdom.[115] It was no surprise, then, on March 4, 2016, that armed fundamentalist extremists breached the compound and killed several of the security personnel and other workers. They systematically searched for and killed four of the sisters as well. But they knew there were five Missionaries of Charity in that place. They searched for the last one, entering the walk-in refrigeration unit she was in several times, but failed to find her. She alone survived to tell the story of what happened on that horrible morning.

---

115. Francesca Pollio Fenton, "6 Years Ago These Religious Sisters Died in Yemen," National Catholic Register, March 7, 2022, https://www.ncregister.com/cna/6-years-ago-these-religious-sisters-died-in-yemen.

The fax report that was sent some twelve hours after the attack gave a detailed explanation of what took place. The surviving sister noted how the Missionaries of Charity were attentive to their promises for prayer and service on the morning of the attack, making it predictable where they would be. But instead of lamenting that fact, the sister expressed a hauntingly beautiful truth that focuses, instead, on Jesus Christ. She said, "Because of their faithfulness, they were in the *right* place at the *right* time and were ready when the Bridegroom came."[116]

When the Bridegroom came . . . She was, of course, making a direct reference to the parable of Christ in the Gospel of Saint Matthew. Jesus tells the story of the ten virgins who are waiting in vigil for the bridegroom's return. Five of them were foolish and did not have enough oil reserved as they waited. They needed to leave their vigil to purchase more. Jesus relates, "And while they went to buy, the bridegroom came, and those who were ready went in with him to the marriage feast; and the door was shut" (Mt 25:10).

The lamps can represent the vitality of our faith—something that cannot be transferred to another person but represents a gift that has to be sought, received, embraced, and lived. We either respond to God's invitation and express our faith in works of charity, or we do not. The oil for those lamps, therefore, stands for the good works our faith inspires. Our

---

116. Joan Frawley Desmond, "Eyewitness Account of ISIS Attack on Mother Teresa's Sisters in Yemen," National Catholic Register, March 17, 2016, https://www.ncregister.com/news/ eyewitness-account-of-isis-attack-on-mother-teresas-sisters-in-yemen.

lamps of faith must always be burning, and the oil of good works must continue to attend us in lives of fidelity throughout this earthly pilgrimage. The message of the Gospel is challenging but beautiful, as it helps us to see that the heart of the Christian faith lies in our relationship with Jesus Christ, the Bridegroom.

Of course, the Bridegroom does not come to us in martyrdom only. He comes to us in all the moments of our lives. In a particular way the Bridegroom comes to us when we are suffering—in our emotional pain, spiritual desolation, and physical ailments small and large. I will never forget a powerful moment in my priestly ministry when I was newly ordained. A man approached me after Mass and told me that his fiancée was dying in the hospital and asked if I would go to visit her. When I arrived at the hospital I braced myself for what I anticipated would be a difficult encounter. Instead, when I entered her room and spoke with her, she was completely serene. She went on to tell me that she had grown in prayer through the suffering she had experienced. In fact, she said, there was a recent moment where she felt that she was in the presence of Christ and that he was calling her home. "I am ready for him," she told me. Whatever challenges and difficulties she had faced up to that point, the Bridegroom had not left her alone nor without hope.

There are two basic points, therefore, that we can reflect on when it comes to the Gospel of Suffering. Firstly, we recall that our Bridegroom weds himself to us in the moment of the Cross. That hatred that caused the Son of God to be crucified is transformed into the act of greatest love and selflessness, God pouring out his life for us in Christ. That is why we call that day "Good Friday." But the night before he suffers and dies, Jesus Christ, in a certain sense, professes "vows" to his Bride, the Church. What are vows? A bridegroom pronounces vows to his spouse when he promises her that he will give himself—body and soul—to her alone; he promises that their love will be fruitful, open to new life; and that he will remain faithful to her until death. Christ gives to the Church, his Bride, his own Body and Blood in the Eucharist at the Last Supper. His vows are fulfilled.

Secondly, we as the Bride of Christ are called to fidelity. We are called to have the light of faith in every aspect of our lives, and to be inspired by that faith to perform good works and love God and those around us. We constantly keep those lamps burning with the sacraments, the teachings of our faith, and the countless ways that God inspires us to love. We seek to grow in virtue and commit ourselves to being faithful disciples, especially when we experience the cross and times are challenging. Above all, we pray and strive for vigilance, to be always ready and watching for Jesus Christ in our daily lives. We pray that we also may be ready "when the bridegroom comes."

1. Have I ever experienced a time when I suffered for my faith in Christ or for being a member of the Church?

2. In moments of suffering, where have I experienced the nearness of Christ? Has this ever taken on an unexpected form?

3. What are some of the ways that I can keep the light of faith burning brightly when I face difficulties and challenges in life?

O GOD, ALMIGHTY FATHER, as we seek to follow Christ we sometimes encounter hostility, difficulties, and the cross. We falter when we encounter so many obstacles and challenges in our lives. Give us courage to live our faith with generosity and hope in the face of our affliction. Help us to experience even now that love that will culminate in union with you for all eternity. We ask this through Jesus Christ, our Lord. Amen.

CHAPTER 20

Suffering with Christ

Listening for God's Voice

In the first days of his captivity, he could hear the ringing of the bells of the cathedral in the city of Nha Trang, where he had previously been bishop. The prison was that close. Far from becoming bitter about that ironic reality, he would later say, "The Father did not abandon me."[117] His deep faith endured through those initial days of trial, and he kept his focus on God.

From the outset there were five guards assigned to Van Thuan; they would take shifts, two at a time, watching over him. At first, the leaders determined to change the groups

---

117. Cardinal Francis Xavier Nguyen Van Thuan, *Testimony of Hope: The Spiritual Exercises of John Paul II*, trans. Julia Mary Darrenkamp, FSP. and Anne Eileen Heffernan, FSP (Boston: Pauline Books and Media, 2000), 88.

completely every two weeks, fearing the guards would become "'contaminated' by this dangerous bishop."[118] Van Thuan said to himself, "You have the love of Christ in your heart; love them as Jesus loved you."[119] The effect on the guards was so powerful that many of them began to consider him a friend and not a prisoner. The leaders then told the guards, "We've decided not to switch you anymore; otherwise this bishop will contaminate all of the police."[120]

In 1988, Van Thuan was finally released from prison. Three years later, realizing how contagious the bishop's faith was, the government "invited" him to leave the country and never come back! He came to Rome, and in 1994 Saint John Paul II appointed him Prefect for the Pontifical Council for Justice and Peace. He was later created a cardinal and served the Church until his death in 2002. In 2017 Pope Francis named him venerable, the first step on the way to becoming a canonized saint. Whether prisoner or prelate, Venerable Francis Xavier Nguyen Van Thuan was always a man totally filled with joy; it overflowed into the lives of those around him.

✠ ✠ ✠

Cardinal Van Thuan could clearly hear the ringing of the bells in the cathedral where he ought to have been preaching the Gospel. He would have heard the derisive voices of his captors on a daily basis. Certainly, after years of captivity, he

---

118. Nguyen Van Thuan, *Testimony of Hope,* 72.

119. Nguyen Van Thuan, *Testimony of Hope,* 72.

120. Nguyen Van Thuan, *Testimony of Hope,* 72.

would have heard the voice of discouragement deep within his heart. What he chose to listen to, instead, was the voice of God. It was tuning in to the voice of God deep within his soul that allowed Van Thuan to love, even when the circumstances of his life were harsh and bitter.

The second "chapter" in the Gospel of Suffering "is written by all those *who suffer together with Christ*, uniting their human sufferings to His salvific suffering."[121] This process of suffering with Christ is not something that happens without a significant struggle. Saint John Paul II places it in terms of a spiritual conversion and uses the example of the saints like Saint Francis of Assisi and Saint Ignatius of Loyola. These were strong men who, early on, had confidence in their earthly abilities and gifts. They each held a certain status in the world that was impressive from a human perspective. Nevertheless, it was in weakness and powerlessness that they were able to find their greatest strength in God. They learned how to listen to the voice of God in the midst of their suffering.

The Apostle Saint Paul is no different. In his Second Letter to the Corinthians, he talks about the visions and revelations he has been given, but then quickly dismisses these as a source of his strength. He talks, instead, about how "a thorn was given me in the flesh," a mysterious affliction that caused him no little suffering (2 Corinthians 12:7). He had begged the Lord to remove that cross. Instead, God responded, "My grace is sufficient for you, for my power is made perfect in weakness" (2 Corinthians 12:9). Therefore, Saint Paul continues to relate, "for the sake of Christ, then, I am content

---

121. Saint John Paul II, *Salvifici Doloris*, no. 26.

with weaknesses, insults, hardships, persecutions, and calamities; for when I am weak, then I am strong" (2 Corinthians 12:10).

This call to deeper conversion in suffering sheds some light on the mystery of suffering and allows us to see why some crosses are not immediately taken away when we call on God for assistance. Saint John Paul II explains how it is almost always the case that the suffering person begins with "a *typically human protest* and *with the question of 'why'*."[122] It can happen that within this process of questioning and protest we begin to perceive the suffering of Christ. The God whom we are questioning did, in great love, suffer on the cross to save us. God does not stand by idly while we alone experience the cross. God himself has come to take on our sufferings in Christ. That does not immediately alleviate our pain or relieve our sorrow, but it does change the way that we look at the question of "why."

When I was in my first year of seminary studies in Providence, Rhode Island, I went through a particularly painful period of growth in the spiritual life. It was a time of much introspection and coming to terms with my many limitations that made it difficult for me to follow the call to charity and humility. One morning I walked to the small chapel on campus where I frequently went to be alone with God. There was in that place an enormous cross with a very realistic corpus on it showing in detail the suffering of the crucified Christ. Looking at that cross, I suddenly said aloud, "Jesus, you look like I feel." After some time in silent prayer, I took out my Bible and wrote the following prayer on the front

---

122. Saint John Paul II, *Salvifici Doloris*, no. 26.

cover: "Lord, I would give anything in the world not to be broken; and yet you gave everything so that you could be, and so that we could be healed."

Conversion, writes Saint John Paul II, often happens over a long period of time, and we should not expect to arrive quickly at the place where our suffering is redemptive and a fruitful sharing in the cross of Christ.[123] Suffering is disheartening, discouraging, and often devastating. Yet we know in faith that Jesus Christ experienced the very same thing. When we begin to pay more attention to the cross of Jesus Christ, we make it possible to hear his voice and sense his call in our suffering. We come to realize that we are not alone; we are loved and cared for. We may even come to realize that he is able to give us strength and courage in the afflictions we face when we need it the most.

We can return once again to the examples of conversion given earlier, those of Saint Francis of Assisi and Saint Ignatius of Loyola. It was from a place of physical and spiritual suffering that Saint Francis of Assisi began to recognize the call of Christ to intimacy and a sharing of the cross. As a young man Francis participated in a military campaign against Perugia and was captured in battle. While imprisoned he became ill and suffered greatly before he was finally ransomed. Once he returned home, he struggled to let go of his former, carefree way of life and to embrace the Gospel. A key moment of conversion for him was seeing a leper and overcoming his natural aversion to the dreaded disease; Francis approached the sick man and kissed him. He would hear Christ speaking to him from the cross in the Church of San Damiano, yet it

---

123. Saint John Paul II, *Salvifici Doloris*, no. 26.

would take many years before he would enter more deeply into that participation in Christ's salvific work of redemption. By the end of his life, though, he became so enamored of the cross that he received the stigmata, the very wounds of Christ, in his feet, his hands, and his side.

Saint Ignatius of Loyola, recuperating in bed from a painful and humiliating battle wound, was also far from living the way of the cross. Over time, however, he would grow in his ability to discern the inner workings of God. Ignatius meditated frequently on the cross of Jesus Christ, imagining himself present at Calvary and conversing with the crucified Christ. These meditations would change him and mold him into a man of the cross, ready to serve the Church with his entire life. This is the meaning of divine grace, the manner in which God takes ordinary persons and transforms them into extraordinary saints.

For all of us, there are moments in our suffering that can become wellsprings for ongoing conversion and a deepening of faith, when God's voice cuts through our turmoil. When I was in my twenties, I volunteered at a local homeless shelter once a week. One evening I came to the shelter with a heavy heart. For about a week I had felt as if God was very distant and prayer was difficult at best. For no apparent reason, I simply felt abandoned and alone in my faith. "Where are you, God?" I prayed, but there was no answer. Toward the end of the evening, a woman who was staying at the shelter asked if I had a moment to talk. She was visibly upset, struggling with the difficult events that had led her to this shelter. I listened attentively as she described one tragic circumstance after another. She was barely able to keep back the tears as she spoke. Suddenly, I felt the presence of God in my soul in a way that was palpable. I did not hear a divine voice or see a vision, but I felt God speaking to my soul, as if to say, "I am here, now. I am standing right in front of you and I am suffering."

Many times it is through our own suffering that we experience conversion and renewal. At other times, however, it could be the suffering of those around us. We live in a world immersed in suffering, and God often speaks to us through the people we encounter every day. We need to ask for the grace to be attentive to the voice of God, whether it comes through our own silent meditation or through the lives of those around us.

How much time do we give to God in silent prayer and meditation on the transforming power of the cross? Are we also capable of discerning the inner workings of divine grace through the people God places in our paths? As it did with all the saints, it will take much time to discover God present in our suffering and to hear his call amid the trials we face. There is no one method or single technique for prayer and growth in the spiritual life. Yet we do all need to be willing to spend time alone with God each day, attentive to his voice in the silence, as well as in the noise of our everyday lives. Conversion is a supernatural experience that necessarily requires the grace of God, but it cannot fully happen without our cooperation and the intense desire to participate in God's awesome and mysterious plan for our lives.

1. When I meditate on conversion, what do I feel God calling me to turn away from or to turn toward at this time in my life?

2. Do I find it more difficult to pray when I am suffering? Have there been times when the experience of suffering has helped me to hear God more clearly?

3. What stirs in me when I hear that Christ wants me to personally take part in his work of redemption? What would a full response to this invitation look like?

O GOD, ALMIGHTY FATHER, the crosses we face in life are often mysterious and overwhelming. We search for meaning and purpose in our trials and we long to experience your consolation and peace. Grant us a deeper faith and trust in you and help us to hear your voice as we follow you on the path of salvation. We ask this in the name of Jesus Christ, our Lord. Amen.

CHAPTER 21

Set Free

The Descending Meaning of Suffering

There is a church in the north of Belgium, in the enchanting town of Bruges, named the Basilica of the Holy Blood. In many ways that church is a monument to the suffering, death, and resurrection of our Lord. It purports to have a vial of the blood of Jesus Christ, obtained from a cloth used by Joseph of Arimathea when the body of Christ was being prepared for burial. The citizens of Bruges organize a procession with the Holy Blood every year, and the basilica itself wonderfully celebrates the passion of Jesus Christ.

In the Lower Basilica, there is a unique statue of Christ in the moments leading up to his crucifixion. Jesus is seated, with a crown of thorns on his head, and his hands are bound with a thick rope. His face, however, is completely serene and regal. That statue clearly communicates what we believe about the passion. Christ is not bound out of weakness, but in great strength he willingly surrenders himself into the hands of men. His being bound is the act of love that sets us free; his death and resurrection are what give us forgiveness and eternal life. Isaiah the Prophet, in his anticipation of Christ as the suffering servant, explains it beautifully:

> "But he was pierced for our sins,
>   crushed for our iniquity.
> He bore the punishment that makes us whole,
>   by his wounds we were healed" (Isaiah 53:5 NABRE).

Because Jesus Christ was bound, we are set free.

✠ ✠ ✠

The free decision to descend into our human suffering to set us free is not something that Jesus chose to do only once. He has bound himself to suffering humanity and continues to work in our lives even now. One of the great insights of Saint John Paul II in *Salvifici Doloris* is that redemptive suffering is a vocation. Taken from the Latin word *vocare*, to call, vocation forms an integral part of every individual Christian journey. We are all called to respond to Jesus Christ in the particular circumstances of our lives. For some, vocation involves a commitment to marriage, priesthood, or religious life. For all of us there is also the call to unite ourselves to Christ and to sanctify our daily lives. This last sense is what Saint John Paul is referring to when he speaks about the vocation of redemptive suffering. It is something deeply personal that descends to the very heart of one who suffers. He writes:

"Christ does not explain in the abstract the reasons for suffering, but before all else He says: 'Follow me!' Come! Take part through your suffering in this work of saving the world, a salvation achieved through my suffering! Through my cross! Gradually, *as the individual takes up his cross*, spiritually uniting himself to the cross of Christ, the salvific meaning of suffering is revealed before him. He does not discover this meaning at his own human level, but at the level of the suffering of Christ. At the same time, however, from this level of Christ the salvific meaning of suffering *descends to man's level* and becomes, in a sense, the individual's personal response. It is then that man finds in his suffering interior peace and even spiritual joy."[124]

God comes to us in our suffering and whispers our name. We discover that we are not alone and that he has found us. He comes close to us and helps us to carry the burden of the cross, but he also invites us to participate in his work of redeeming the world. Far from being bound by our suffering and helpless, we can become instruments of grace in the lives of those around us.

I witnessed a powerful example of this during my first parish assignment. I was caring for a woman who was suffering from an incurable illness that left her more and more debilitated every week. At one point she asked me to explain to her the Church's teaching on the communion of saints. I spoke about how the Church triumphant in heaven intercedes for us as we struggle through life, and how the souls in purgatory rely on our prayers and sacrifices to help them in their need. "Finally," she responded, "I see that I can contribute in some way to the good of others." She realized that

---

124. Saint John Paul II, *Salvifici Doloris*, no. 26.

her suffering could be helpful, if offered to Christ in love, to assist the souls in purgatory that were being purified and made ready for heaven. She was answering a call from God to unite herself more completely to the redemptive work of Christ.

In his first Apostolic Exhortation, *Evangelii Gaudium*, Pope Francis relates how the Holy Spirit is still at work in the lives of all people, helping to unbind them from the complications and complexities of daily life. He explains how we participate in that work of unbinding those around us through our cooperation with God: "To believe that the Holy Spirit is at work in everyone means realizing that he seeks to penetrate every human situation and all social bonds: 'The Holy Spirit can be said to possess an infinite creativity, proper to the divine mind, which knows how to loosen the knots of human affairs, even the most complex and inscrutable'."[125] Of course, God does not set us free without our active cooperation in his grace and mercy. The Holy Spirit helps to loosen the knots that have held us bound, but we need to be willing to enter freely into that process. In the Gospel of Saint John, Jesus raises Lazarus from the dead, but then tells those who witnessed that great miracle, "Unbind him, and let him go" (Jn 11:44).

We encounter Christ in our suffering, he who gives us true freedom and new life. We are then motivated to intercede for the suffering persons around us, allowing the Holy Spirit to "loosen the knots" of others. We do not have to wait until we have been healed of our own infirmities in order to reach

125. Pope Francis, *Evangelii Gaudium*, no. 178.

out as wounded healers to help those around us. We are called both to receive the healing grace of Christ when we are afflicted and also to reach out to others with acts of love that will help alleviate their suffering. This is the great legacy of the Church, and we are all responsible for how well or how poorly we cooperate in this magnificent work. In Saint Matthew's Gospel of the Last Judgment, the evangelist reminds us that the ones who are bound by poverty, thirst, hunger, loneliness, and whatever social bonds oppress them are, ultimately, Christ in a *distressing disguise*, to use a favorite expression of Saint Teresa of Calcutta.

The Cathedral of Notre Dame in Paris has a captivating depiction of this scene from Saint Matthew's Gospel. The central doorway, containing the "Portal of the Last Judgement," shows Christ the King, seated on his royal throne. Below him is Saint Michael the Archangel, weighing the lives of all in the balance. Those who have responded well to Christ and have been judged worthy of eternal life are on Christ's right, ready to join the saints and angels forever. Those found wanting, however, are lined up on his left. They are being corralled by two demons, one on each end of the line, holding a rope that guides the condemned to their demise. The rope, however, is not tied to any one of them. It rests by their side, as if they could simply step over it, or slip under the rope at any minute and return to Jesus Christ. The point the sculptor wanted to make is that these souls were perfectly free all throughout their lives to answer the call of God. They were always free to recognize him in need and do something to respond to their neighbor, but they freely chose not to do so.

Pope Francis explains Matthew's Last Judgment, and similar passages, by stating, "What these passages make clear is the absolute priority of 'going forth from ourselves towards our brothers and sisters.'"[126] This, he indicates, is the love that Christ commands, that same love that is the foundation for every moral norm and a sign of our spiritual growth in Christ.

God lovingly chooses to set us free from our sins, helping us overcome many of the complications of life and welcoming us into friendship with himself. He was bound and suffered death that we might enter eternal life. But, Pope Francis reminds us, there is an "absolute priority" for us, in having received so great a gift, to reach out to those around us in the name of Jesus Christ. From the beginning of his papacy, Pope Francis has called the Church to recognize and reach out to those "on the peripheries," those who find themselves on the outside. As he describes in *Evangelii Gaudium*, "Our faith in Christ, who became poor, and was always close to the poor and the outcast, is the basis of our concern for the integral development of society's most neglected members."[127] We are called to identify and assist those on the peripheries, whatever those might look like in our families, neighborhoods, and communities. According to our fidelity in this regard, we will be judged. Saint John of the Cross put it most eloquently when he wrote that, at the twilight of life, we will be judged by love.

Suffering has a way of finding us, whether we are ready for it or not. God, too, seeks us out and descends into our suffering in order to give us eternal life and untie the knots that bind us. What a comfort, to know that we are not alone in our suffering, not bound by the crosses that afflict us. By Christ's

---

126. Pope Francis, *Evangelii Gaudium*, no. 179.
127. Pope Francis, *Evangelii Gaudium*, no. 186.

wounds we are healed and set free. "In the messianic program of Christ," writes Saint John Paul II, "which is at the same time the program *of the kingdom of God*, suffering is present in the world in order to release love, in order to give birth to works of love toward neighbor, in order to transform the whole of human civilization into a 'civilization of love.'"[128] The reality of suffering reveals the world as it is, but our response to suffering can help form the world into something completely different. Cooperating with Christ and uniting our suffering with his, we can participate in his work of annihilating evil and creating good.

1. How is God calling to me in my suffering today?

2. What are some of the ways that I feel inspired to help unbind and loosen the knots of those around me?

3. As I continue to contend with the mystery of suffering in my life, what is one concrete resolution I desire to make for the journey ahead?

O GOD, ALMIGHTY FATHER, you sent your only-begotten Son to suffer and die to save us from our sins. We long to enter more completely into that salvation and to be set free from the bonds that keep us from living a full Christian life. Help us to cooperate with your grace and experience your healing in our lives. May we become your instruments in the lives of those around us. We ask this in the name of Jesus Christ, our Lord. Amen.

---

128. Saint John Paul II, *Salvifici Doloris*, no. 30.

Acknowledgments

Appendices

Sacred Scripture on Suffering and Hope

It is the LORD who goes before you; he will be with you, he will not fail you or forsake you; do not fear or be dismayed.

— DEUTERONOMY 31:8

✠ ✠ ✠

Have I not commanded you? Be strong and of good courage; be not frightened, neither be dismayed; for the LORD your God is with you wherever you go.

— JOSHUA 1:9

✠ ✠ ✠

How long, O LORD? Wilt thou forget me for ever?
    How long wilt thou hide thy face from me?
How long must I bear pain in my soul,
    and have sorrow in my heart all the day?
How long shall my enemy be exalted over me?

Consider and answer me, O LORD my God;
    lighten my eyes, lest I sleep the sleep of death;
lest my enemy say, "I have prevailed over him";
    lest my foes rejoice because I am shaken.

But I have trusted in thy steadfast love;
    my heart shall rejoice in thy salvation.
I will sing to the LORD,
    because he has dealt bountifully with me.

— PSALM 13

✠ ✠ ✠

The LORD is my shepherd, I shall not want;
    he makes me lie down in green pastures.
He leads me beside still waters;
    he restores my soul.
He leads me in paths of righteousness
    for his name's sake.

Even though I walk through the valley of the shadow of death,
    I fear no evil;
for thou art with me;
    thy rod and thy staff,
    they comfort me.

Thou preparest a table before me
    in the presence of my enemies;

thou anointest my head with oil,
>   my cup overflows.
Surely goodness and mercy shall follow me
>   all the days of my life;
and I shall dwell in the house of the LORD
>   for ever.

— PSALM 23

✠ ✠ ✠

Vindicate me, O God, and defend my cause
>   against an ungodly people;
from deceitful and unjust men
>   deliver me!
For thou art the God in whom I take refuge;
>   why hast thou cast me off?
Why go I mourning
>   because of the oppression of the enemy?

Oh send out thy light and thy truth;
>   let them lead me,
let them bring me to thy holy hill
>   and to thy dwelling!
Then I will go to the altar of God,
>   to God my exceeding joy;
and I will praise thee with the lyre,
>   O God, my God.

Why are you cast down, O my soul,
>   and why are you disquieted within me?
Hope in God; for I shall again praise him,
>   my help and my God.

— PSALM 43

✠ ✠ ✠

He who dwells in the shelter of the Most High,
        who abides in the shadow of the Almighty,
will say to the LORD, "My refuge and my fortress;
        my God, in whom I trust."
For he will deliver you from the snare of the fowler
        and from the deadly pestilence;
he will cover you with his pinions,
        and under his wings you will find refuge;
        his faithfulness is a shield and buckler.
You will not fear the terror of the night,
        nor the arrow that flies by day,
nor the pestilence that stalks in darkness,
        nor the destruction that wastes at noonday.

A thousand may fall at your side,
        ten thousand at your right hand;
        but it will not come near you.
You will only look with your eyes
        and see the recompense of the wicked.

Because you have made the Lord your refuge,
        the Most High your habitation,
no evil shall befall you,
        no scourge come near your tent.

For he will give his angels charge of you
        to guard you in all your ways.
On their hands they will bear you up,
        lest you dash your foot against a stone.
You will tread on the lion and the adder,
        the young lion and the serpent you will trample
                under foot.

Because he cleaves to me in love, I will deliver him;
　　I will protect him, because he knows my name.
When he calls to me, I will answer him;
　　I will be with him in trouble,
　　I will rescue him and honor him.
With long life I will satisfy him,
　　and show him my salvation.

— Psalm 91

I lift up my eyes to the hills.
From whence does my help come?
My help comes from the Lord,
　　who made heaven and earth.

He will not let your foot be moved,
　　he who keeps you will not slumber.
Behold, he who keeps Israel
　　will neither slumber nor sleep.

The Lord is your keeper;
　　the Lord is your shade
　　on your right hand.
The sun shall not smite you by day,
　　nor the moon by night.

The Lord will keep you from all evil;
　　he will keep your life.
The Lord will keep
　　your going out and your coming in
　　from this time forth and for evermore.

— Psalm 121

✠ ✠ ✠

Out of the depths I cry to thee, O Lord!
    Lord, hear my voice!
Let thy ears be attentive
    to the voice of my supplications!

If thou, O Lord, shouldst mark iniquities,
    Lord, who could stand?
But there is forgiveness with thee,
    that thou mayest be feared.

I wait for the Lord, my soul waits,
    and in his word I hope;
my soul waits for the Lord
    more than watchmen for the morning,
    more than watchmen for the morning.

O Israel, hope in the Lord!
    For with the Lord there is steadfast love,
    and with him is plenteous redemption.
And he will redeem Israel
    from all his iniquities.

                    — Psalm 130

✠ ✠ ✠

Why do you say, O Jacob,
    and speak, O Israel,
"My way is hid from the Lord,
    and my right is disregarded by my God"?
Have you not known? Have you not heard?
The Lord is the everlasting God,
    the Creator of the ends of the earth.
He does not faint or grow weary,

his understanding is unsearchable.
He gives power to the faint,
    and to him who has no might he increases strength.
Even youths shall faint and be weary,
    and young men shall fall exhausted;
but they who wait for the shall renew their strength,
    they shall mount up with wings like eagles,
they shall run and not be weary,
    they shall walk and not faint.

— Isaiah 40:27–31

Fear not, for I am with you,
    be not dismayed, for I am your God;
I will strengthen you, I will help you,
    I will uphold you with my victorious right hand.

— Isaiah 41:10

Fear not, for I am with you,

But now thus says the Lord,
he who created you, O Jacob,
    he who formed you, O Israel:
"Fear not, for I have redeemed you;
    I have called you by name, you are mine.
When you pass through the waters I will be with you;
    and through the rivers, they shall not overwhelm you;
when you walk through fire you shall not be burned,
    and the flame shall not consume you."

— Isaiah 43:1–2

✠ ✠ ✠

But Zion said, "The Lord has forsaken me,
    my Lord has forgotten me."
"Can a woman forget her sucking child,
    that she should have no compassion on the son of her
    womb?
Even these may forget,
    yet I will not forget you.
Behold, I have graven you on the palms of my hands;
    your walls are continually before me."

— Isaiah 49:14–16

✠ ✠ ✠

"O afflicted one, storm-tossed, and not comforted,
    behold, I will set your stones in antimony,
    and lay your foundations with sapphires.
I will make your pinnacles of agate,
    your gates of carbuncles,
    and all your wall of precious stones.
All your sons shall be taught by the Lord,
    and great shall be the prosperity of your sons.
In righteousness you shall be established;
    you shall be far from oppression, for you shall not fear;
    and from terror, for it shall not come near you."

— Isaiah 54:11–14

✠ ✠ ✠

For I know the plans I have for you, says the Lord, plans
for welfare and not for evil, to give you a future and a hope.

Then you will call upon me and come and pray to me, and I will hear you. You will seek me and find me; when you seek me with all your heart.

— JEREMIAH 29:11–13

✠ ✠ ✠

I have loved you with an everlasting love;
     therefore I have continued my faithfulness to you.

— JEREMIAH 31:3

✠ ✠ ✠

Remember my affliction and my bitterness,
     the wormwood and the gall!
My soul continually thinks of it
     and is bowed down within me.
But this I call to mind,
     and therefore I have hope:

The steadfast love of the LORD never ceases,
     his mercies never come to an end;
they are new every morning;
     great is thy faithfulness.
"The LORD is my portion," says my soul,
     "therefore I will hope in him."

— LAMENTATIONS 3:19–24

✠ ✠ ✠

"Blessed are the poor in spirit, for theirs is the kingdom of heaven.

"Blessed are those who mourn, for they shall be comforted.

"Blessed are the meek, for they shall inherit the earth.

"Blessed are those who hunger and thirst for righteousness, for they shall be satisfied.

"Blessed are the merciful, for they shall obtain mercy.

"Blessed are the pure in heart, for they shall see God.

"Blessed are the peacemakers, for they shall be called sons of God.

"Blessed are those who are persecuted for righteousness' sake, for theirs is the kingdom of heaven.

"Blessed are you when men revile you and persecute you and utter all kinds of evil against you falsely on my account. Rejoice and be glad, for your reward is great in heaven, for so men persecuted the prophets who were before you."

— MATTHEW 5:3–12

✠ ✠ ✠

"Come to me, all who labor and are heavy laden, and I will give you rest. Take my yoke upon you, and learn from me; for I am gentle and lowly in heart, and you will find rest for your souls. For my yoke is easy, and my burden is light."

— MATTHEW 11:28–30

✠ ✠ ✠

"Peace I leave with you; my peace I give to you; not as the world gives do I give to you. Let not your hearts be troubled, neither let them be afraid."

— JOHN 14:27

✠ ✠ ✠

"I have said this to you, that in me you may have peace. In the world you have tribulation; but be of good cheer, I have overcome the world."

— JOHN 16:33

✠ ✠ ✠

Therefore, since we are justified by faith, we have peace with God through our Lord Jesus Christ. Through him we have obtained access to this grace in which we stand, and we rejoice in our hope of sharing the glory of God. More than that, we rejoice in our sufferings, knowing that suffering produces endurance, and endurance produces character, and character produces hope, and hope does not disappoint us, because God's love has been poured into our hearts through the Holy Spirit who has been given to us.

— ROMANS 5:1–5

✠ ✠ ✠

I consider that the sufferings of this present time are not worth comparing with the glory that is to be revealed to us.

— ROMANS 8:18

✠ ✠ ✠

Blessed be the God and Father of our Lord Jesus Christ, the Father of mercies and God of all comfort, who comforts us in all our affliction, so that we may be able to comfort those who are in any affliction, with the comfort with which we ourselves are comforted by God.

— 2 CORINTHIANS 1:3–4

✠ ✠ ✠

But we have this treasure in earthen vessels, to show that the transcendent power belongs to God and not to us. We are afflicted in every way, but not crushed; perplexed, but not driven to despair; persecuted, but not forsaken; struck down, but not destroyed; always carrying in the body the death of Jesus, so that the life of Jesus may also be manifested in our bodies.

— 2 Corinthians 4:7–10

✠ ✠ ✠

I have been crucified with Christ; it is no longer I who live, but Christ who lives in me; and the life I now live in the flesh I live by faith in the Son of God, who loved me and gave himself for me.

— Galatians 2:20

✠ ✠ ✠

Have this mind among yourselves, which was in Christ Jesus, who, though he was in the form of God, did not count equality with God a thing to be grasped, but emptied himself, taking the form of a servant, being born in the likeness of men. And being found in human form he humbled himself and became obedient unto death, even death on a cross. Therefore God has highly exalted him and bestowed on him the name which is above every name, that at the name of Jesus every knee should bow, in heaven and on earth and under the earth, and every tongue confess that Jesus Christ is Lord, to the glory of God the Father.

— Philippians 2:5–11

✠ ✠ ✠

I want to know Christ and the power of his resurrection and the sharing of his sufferings by becoming like him in his death, if somehow I may attain the resurrection from the dead.

— Philippians 3:10–11 NRSV

✠ ✠ ✠

Have no anxiety about anything, but in everything by prayer and supplication with thanksgiving let your requests be made known to God. And the peace of God, which passes all understanding, will keep your hearts and your minds in Christ Jesus.

— Philippians 4:6–7

✠ ✠ ✠

Now I rejoice in my sufferings for your sake, and in my flesh I complete what is lacking in Christ's afflictions for the sake of his body, that is, the church.

— Colossians 1:24

✠ ✠ ✠

Therefore, since we are surrounded by so great a cloud of witnesses, let us also lay aside every weight, and sin which clings so closely, and let us run with perseverance the race that is set before us, looking to Jesus the pioneer and perfecter of our faith, who for the joy that was set before him endured the cross, despising the shame, and is seated at the right hand of the throne of God.

— Hebrews 12:1–2

✠ ✠ ✠

Count it all joy, my brethren, when you meet various trials, for you know that the testing of your faith produces steadfastness. And let steadfastness have its full effect, that you may be perfect and complete, lacking in nothing.

—James 1:2–4

✠ ✠ ✠

Beloved, do not be surprised at the fiery ordeal which comes upon you to prove you, as though something strange were happening to you. But rejoice in so far as you share Christ's sufferings, that you may also rejoice and be glad when his glory is revealed.

— 1 Peter 4:12–13

✠ ✠ ✠

Humble yourselves therefore under the mighty hand of God, that in due time he may exalt you. Cast all your anxieties on him, for he cares about you.

— 1 Peter 5:6–7

✠ ✠ ✠

Then I saw a new heaven and a new earth; for the first heaven and the first earth had passed away, and the sea was no more. And I saw the holy city, new Jerusalem, coming down out of heaven from God, prepared as a bride adorned for her husband; and I heard a great voice from the throne saying, "Behold, the dwelling of God is with men. He will dwell with them, and they shall be his people, and God himself will be with them; he will wipe away every tear from their eyes, and death shall be no more, neither shall there be mourning nor crying nor pain any more, for the former things have passed away."

And he who sat upon the throne said, "Behold, I make all things new."

— REVELATION 21:1–5

Appendix II

Prayers for Times of Suffering

Memorare

Remember, O most gracious Virgin Mary, that never was it known that anyone who fled to thy protection, implored thy help, or sought thy intercession, was left unaided. Inspired by this confidence I fly unto thee, O Virgin of virgins, my Mother. To thee do I come, before thee I stand, sinful and sorrowful. O Mother of the Word Incarnate, despise not my petitions, but in thy mercy hear and answer me. Amen.

Prayer to Saint Michael the Archangel

Saint Michael, the Archangel, defend us in battle; be our defense against the wickedness and snares of the devil. May God rebuke him, we humbly pray; and do thou, O Prince of the heavenly host, by the power of God, thrust into hell Satan and the other evil spirits who prowl about the world seeking the ruin of souls. Amen.

Prayer to One's Guardian Angel

Angel of God, my guardian dear, to whom His love commits me here. Ever this day be at my side, to light and guard, to rule and guide. Amen.

Lead Kindly Light

Saint John Henry Newman, 1801–1890

Lead, Kindly Light, amidst th'encircling gloom,
Lead Thou me on!
The night is dark, and I am far from home,
Lead Thou me on!
Keep Thou my feet; I do not ask to see
The distant scene; one step enough for me.

I was not ever thus, nor prayed that Thou
Shouldst lead me on;
I loved to choose and see my path; but now
Lead Thou me on!

I loved the garish day, and, spite of fears,
Pride ruled my will. Remember not past years!

So long Thy power hath blest me, sure it still
Will lead me on.
O'er moor and fen, o'er crag and torrent, till
The night is gone,
And with the morn those angel faces smile,
Which I have loved long since, and lost awhile!

Prayer of Saint Teresa of Avila

Let nothing disturb you.
Let nothing frighten you.
All things pass.
God never changes.
Patience obtains all things.
He who has God lacks nothing.
God alone suffices.

Prayer Before the Crucifix

Saint Francis of Assisi, 1181–1226

Most High, glorious God,
enlighten the darkness of my heart and give me
true faith, certain hope, and perfect charity,
sense and knowledge, Lord, that I may carry out
Your holy and true command. Amen.

I Am Desperate

Saint Anselm of Canterbury, ca. 1033–1109

I am desperate for your love, Lord. My heart is aflame with fervent passion. When I remember the good things you have done, my heart burns with desire to embrace you. I thirst for you; I hunger for you; I long for you; I sigh for you. I am jealous of your love. What shall I say to you? What can I do for you? Where shall I seek you? I am sick for your love. The joy of my heart turns to dust. My happy laughter is reduced to ashes. I want you. I hope for you. My soul is like a widow, bereft of you. Turn to me, and see my tears. Come now, Lord, and I will be comforted. Show me your face, and I shall be saved. Enter my room, and I shall be satisfied. Reveal your beauty, and my joy will be complete.

An Easter Oblation

Fr. Christopher Mahar

She had listened with wonder
To the words of the prophet
About swords piercing,
Battling kingdoms falling
And rising, hearts revealed
To heaven and earth

Meanings lay deep within
As suddenly her heart broke open
To see life wrapped in death
Eternity expended in time, her
Redeemer at her breast, breathless

Dawn slept then in the darkness
Of earth while faith gently taught
Love where to turn and how to hope
Offering herself in sweet labor,
Remembering the promises
Of ages and fathers and children
Set firmly upon an undying word:
Again

APRIL 9, 2012

The Way of the Cross

By Blessed James Alberione (adapted)

V. We adore you, O Christ and we bless you.
R. Because by your cross you have redeemed the world.

Let us pray.

O Lord, look upon your family, for whose sake our Lord Jesus Christ unhesitatingly suffered betrayal into the hands of the wicked and underwent the torment of the cross. Who lives and reigns with you forever and ever. Amen.

Act of Contrition

My most merciful Jesus, kneeling before you, I ask pardon with all my heart for my sins, which I especially deplore and detest because they are an offense to your infinite goodness. I resolve to choose to die rather than to offend you again, even more, I resolve to love you above all things until death.

Have mercy on us, O Lord.
Have mercy on us.

Holy Mother, pierce me through; in my heart, each wound renew of my Savior crucified.

At the cross her station keeping, stood the mournful Mother weeping, close to Jesus to the last.

The First Station

We adore you, O Christ, etc.

The innocent Jesus accepts for the glory of God and peace to humanity, the unjust sentence of death pronounced against him by Pilate.

Most loving Jesus, for your love and in penance for my sins, I accept my death with all the pain and sorrow that will accompany it. May your will and not mine be done, O Lord.

Have mercy on us, etc.

Holy Mother, etc.

Through her heart his sorrow sharing, all his bitter anguish bearing, now at length the sword had passed.

The Second Station

We adore you, O Christ, etc.

Jesus takes the cross upon his shoulders. Jesus Master invites us: "If anyone wishes to come after me, let him deny himself, take up his cross and follow me."

I want to follow you, O Divine Master, by denying myself and accepting my daily cross. Draw me to yourself, O Lord. The road is narrow, but it leads to heaven. Jesus, be my guide and my comfort on my journey through life.

Have mercy on us, etc.

Holy Mother, etc.

Oh, how sad and sore distressed was that Mother highly blest of the sole-begotten one!

The Third Station

We adore you, O Christ, etc.

Wearied by the agony of Gethsemane, tortured by the scourging and the crowning with thorns, exhausted by fasting, Jesus falls for the first time beneath the enormous weight of the cross.

Jesus fell to sustain those who fall. Lead us not into temptation, O Lord, but deliver us from all evil.

Have mercy on us, etc.

Holy Mother, etc.

Christ above in torment hangs; she beneath beholds the pangs of her dying glorious Son.

THE FOURTH STATION

We adore you, O Christ, etc.

Carrying the cross, Jesus meets his Mother, whose soul is pierced by a sword of sorrow. The hearts of Jesus and Mary are united in the same suffering.

Behold the two hearts that have so greatly loved all people. O most sacred hearts of Jesus and Mary, I offer you my whole heart that it may always be yours.

Have mercy on us, etc.

Holy Mother, etc.

Is there one who would not weep, 'whelmed in miseries so deep, Christ's dear Mother to behold?

THE FIFTH STATION

We adore you, O Christ, etc.

With false compassion, the soldiers forced a certain passer-by, Simon of Cyrene, to take up the cross of Jesus.

I too am called to cooperate in the redemption of the world, completing with my sufferings the passion of Jesus Christ (cf. Col 1:24). Accept my small offerings, O good Master, and purify them in your love.

Have mercy on us, etc.

Holy Mother, etc.

Can the human heart refrain from partaking in her pain, in that Mother's pain untold?

The Sixth Station

We adore you, O Christ, etc.

With heartfelt compassion, Veronica wipes the face of Jesus, and he rewards her by leaving the impression of his face on the towel.

I see in this devout disciple the model of those who offer atonement for sins. I ask you, O Lord, for a spirit of penance in order to make reparation for my sins and for the sins of others. O Jesus, grant me a share in the virtues you practiced while you lived on earth.

Have mercy on us, etc.

Holy Mother, etc.

Bruised, derided, cursed, defiled, she beheld her tender child all with bloody scourges rent.

The Seventh Station

We adore you, O Christ, etc.

A second time, Jesus's strength fails him and he who was "a man of suffering" (Is 53:3) falls a second time beneath the cross.

O good Master, thus do you atone for our repeated sins, committed either deliberately or out of weakness. Lord, I repent of my sins. Help me to avoid all sin in the future.

Have mercy on us, etc.

Holy Mother, etc.

For the sins of his own nation she saw him hang in desolation till his spirit forth he sent.

The Eighth Station

We adore you, O Christ, etc.

A large crowd and many women who were weeping for him, followed Jesus. He said to them: "Daughters of Jerusalem, weep not for me but for yourselves and for your children" (Lk 23:28).

I humble myself for my many sins and for those which others have committed because of my bad example and negligence. My Jesus, grant me the grace to help others avoid sin, through my actions, example, word, and prayer.

Have mercy on us, etc.

Holy Mother, etc.

O my Mother, fount of love, touch my spirit from above; make my heart with yours accord.

The Ninth Station

We adore you, O Christ, etc.

Jesus falls the third time beneath the cross. The weight crushes him and he can hardly get up.

When I keep falling into the same sin, Lord, give me the strength to break away from it. Help me to avoid sin in the future and to be faithful to the grace you offer me to follow in all things.

Have mercy on us, etc.

Holy Mother, etc.

Make me feel as you have felt, make my soul to glow and melt with the love of Christ my Lord.

The Tenth Station

We adore you, O Christ, etc.

Having reached Calvary, Jesus is stripped of his garments and given a bitter mixture of gall and myrrh to drink.

Jesus, you suffered so much for us! Keep my heart free of anything that would lead me away from you. Grant me the grace to seek you only, my supreme and eternal happiness.

Have mercy on us, etc.
Holy Mother, etc.

Holy Mother, pierce me through; in my heart each wound renew of my Savior crucified.

The Eleventh Station

We adore you, O Christ, etc.

The executioners nail Jesus to the cross beneath the gaze of his most sorrowful Mother, causing him unspeakable agony.

Jesus, thank you for giving your life for us. I want to be your disciple always. O Jesus, do not let me separate myself from you.

Have mercy on us, etc.
Holy Mother, etc.

Let me share with you his pain, who for all my sins was slain, who for me in torment died.

The Twelfth Station

We adore you, O Christ, etc.

Jesus suffers indescribable pains for three hours and then dies on the cross for our sins.

The death of Jesus is renewed every day on our altars in holy Mass. Most loving Jesus, grant me devotion to holy Mass. May I participate in it often and with the dispositions that your Holy Mother had at the foot of the cross.

Have mercy on us, etc.

Holy Mother, etc.

Let me mingle tears with you, mourning him who mourned for me all the days that I may live.

THE THIRTEENTH STATION

We adore you, O Christ, etc.

The sorrowful Mary receives her Son into her arms, after he was taken down from the cross.

Mary contemplates the wounds of Jesus with immense sorrow and love, and offers her suffering in union with his.

O Mother, accept me as your child. Accompany me throughout my life. Assist me daily and especially in the hour of my death.

Have mercy on us, etc.

Holy Mother, etc.

By the cross with you to stay, there with you to weep and pray, is all I ask of you to give.

THE FOURTEENTH STATION

We adore you, O Christ, etc.

The body of Jesus, anointed with spices, is brought to the sepulcher. With strong faith, Mary awaited the resurrection of her Son, as he had foretold.

I firmly believe, my God, in the resurrection of Jesus Christ, as I believe in the resurrection of the dead. Every day

I want to arise to a new life so as to merit to arise in the glory of the last day.

Have mercy on us, etc.

Holy Mother, etc.

While my body here decays, may my soul your goodness praise, safe in paradise with you. Amen.

V. Save us, O Christ our Savior, through the power of your cross.

R. You who saved Peter on the sea, have mercy on us.

Let us pray.

O God, you sanctified the standard of the life-bestowing cross with the precious blood of your only begotten Son. Grant that those who joyfully honor the holy cross may everywhere rejoice in your protection. Through the same Christ, our Lord. Amen.

Further Resources on Suffering

Paul Chaloux. *Why All People Suffer: How a Loving God Uses Suffering to Perfect Us*. Manchester: Sophia Institute Press, 2021.

Kris Frank. *Hope Always: Our Anchor in Life's Storms*. Pauline Books & Media, 2020.

Victor E. Frankl. *Man's Search for Meaning*. Boston, Beacon Press, 2006.

Benedict J. Groeschel, CFR. *Arise from Darkness: What to Do When Life Doesn't Make Sense*. San Francisco: Ignatius Press, 1995.

Kathryn Hermes, FSP. *Reclaim Regret: How God Heals Life's Disappointments*. Boston: Pauline Books & Media, 2018.

Saint John Paul II. *On the Christian Meaning of Human Suffering*. Anniversary Edition with commentary by Myles Sheehan. Boston: Pauline Books & Media, 2014.

Peter Kreeft. *Making Sense Out of Suffering*. Ann Arbor: Servant Books, 1986.

C. S. Lewis. *The Problem of Pain*. New York: HarperOne, 2015.

Henri J. M. Nouwen. *The Wounded Healer: Ministry in Contemporary Society*. New York: Image Doubleday, 1979.

Philippe de la Trinité. *What Is Redemption: How Christ's Suffering Saves Us*. Steubenville: Emmaus Road Publishing, 2021.

Margaret M. Turek. *Atonement: Soundings in Biblical, Trinitarian, and Spiritual Theology*. San Francisco: Ignatius Press, 2022.

Leonora Wilson, FSP. *Essential Healing Prayers for Peace and Strength*. Boston: Pauline Books & Media, 2021.

BOOKS & MEDIA

A mission of the Daughters of St. Paul

As apostles of Jesus Christ,
evangelizing today's world:

We are CALLED to holiness
by God's living Word and Eucharist.

We COMMUNICATE the Gospel message
through our lives and through all
available forms of media.

We SERVE the Church
by responding to the hopes and needs
of all people with the Word of God,
in the spirit of St. Paul.

For more information visit us at:
www.pauline.org